Bright.

Paulette Mommae Moor

GHOST · BOX

About the Authors

Christopher Moon had his first paranormal experience at the age of seven. At the age of thirteen, he discovered his psychic ability, and thus began his life journey of researching and investigating the paranormal. He has become a fixture at various metaphysical and paranormal conventions around the United States and Canada.

Paulette Moon has traveled the world with her son Chris since 2003, conducing paranormal investigations, classes and lectures, psychic galleries, private readings, and bringing the Moon Family Psychic Experience to colleges and universities. Paulette has been featured on many television networks including FOX and the ABC Family channel. She co-stars on the hit YouTube web series "The Ghost Box Chronicles" with her son Chris.

GHOST · BOX

Voices from Spirits, ETs, Shadow People & Other Astral Beings

CHRIS MOON & PAULETTE MOON

Llewellyn Publications
Woodbury, Minnesota

Ghost Box: Voices from Spirits, ETs, Shadow People & Other Astral Beings © 2017 by Chris Moon and Paulette Moon. All rights reserved. No part of this book may be used or reproduced in any manner whatsoever, including Internet usage, without written permission from Llewellyn Publications, except in the case of brief quotations embodied in critical articles and reviews.

FIRST EDITION
First Printing, 2017

Cover design: Kevin R. Brown
Interior photographs courtesy of the authors except photo on page 135, which is courtesy of Angela Scarpino

Llewellyn Publications is a registered trademark of Llewellyn Worldwide Ltd.

Library of Congress Cataloging-in-Publication Data
Names: Moon, Chris, author.
Title: Ghost box : voices from spirits, ETs, shadow people & other astral beings / Chris Moon and Paulette Moon.
Description: First Edition. | Woodbury : Llewellyn Worldwide, Ltd., 2017.
Identifiers: LCCN 2017027027 (print) | LCCN 2017014164 (ebook) | ISBN 9780738752945 (ebook) | ISBN 9780738751054 (alk. paper)
Subjects: LCSH: Parapsychology—Research.
Classification: LCC BF1040.5 (print) | LCC BF1040.5 .M66 2017 (ebook) | DDC 130—dc23
LC record available at https://lccn.loc.gov/2017027027

Llewellyn Worldwide Ltd. does not participate in, endorse, or have any authority or responsibility concerning private business transactions between our authors and the public.

All mail addressed to the author is forwarded but the publisher cannot, unless specifically instructed by the author, give out an address or phone number.

Any internet references contained in this work are current at publication time, but the publisher cannot guarantee that a specific location will continue to be maintained. Please refer to the publisher's website for links to authors' websites and other sources.

Llewellyn Publications
A Division of Llewellyn Worldwide Ltd.
2143 Wooddale Drive
Woodbury, MN 55125-2989
www.llewellyn.com

Printed in the United States of America

This book is dedicated to the memory of our friend, the late great Frank Sumption. Frank was a creative genius who was dedicated to his craft. His research and contributions to the field of spirit communication revolutionized the profession.

This book is a true recollection and account of ghostly or paranormal phenomena that my mom and I have experienced. We wrote the book together, but the stories are told from my perspective. This account represents, to the best of our ability, actual retellings of real events. Some of the names in the book have been changed for privacy.

Contents

Prologue xi

Foreword xiii

Introduction 1

Chapter One: Frank Sumption and Edison's Telephone to the Dead ... 13

Chapter Two: Sallie House ... 29

Chapter Three: Spooky Childhood and Haunted Times ... 55

Chapter Four: Lizzie Borden House ... 71

Chapter Five: The Bereaved Mothers Club ... 89

Chapter Six: ETs, Shadow People, and Other Strangeness ... 97

Chapter Seven: JFK and Jackie Kennedy at the Grassy Knoll ... 113

Chapter Eight: A Gangster, a President, and Other Ghouls in Illinois ... 123

Chapter Nine: Unsolved Murders at the Lumber Baron Inn ... 133

Chapter Ten: Private Ghost Box Readings, Gallery Readings, and College Tour Stories ... 179

Epilogue 195

Prologue

As I lay there in Mr. Borden's room in the Lizzie Borden house, my eyes quickly adjusted to the dark and I could see streetlights shining in, illuminating small aspects of the corners of the room. I stared up at the ceiling in complete shock and disbelief at the rage- and profanity-filled exchange I'd had earlier that evening via Frank's Box with the spirit of Lizzie Borden's father, Andrew.

After a while, fatigue took over and I tried to get comfortable in the bed. As I rolled over onto my left side, I clearly heard a man's voice whisper: *Don't turn your back!* Once I started breathing again, I tried to calm down, attempting to convince myself that it was my imagination. I thought about where I was, the site of a double axe-murder homicide—not to mention the disturbing, emotionally charged confrontation I'd had with Mr. Borden downstairs and in whose room I was now attempting to sleep. After a few minutes of lying there, I decided to attempt sleep again, this time on my right side. As I was drifting off, I felt a cold breath on my ear and heard a more emphatic warning: *Don't turn your back!* I slept on my back that night.

At some point during the night I woke to my own desperate gasps for air. Something tightened around my throat, cutting off my air supply—but when I reached out for whatever it was, there was nothing. Panicked, I sat up and started lashing out at the air around me, falling out of bed in my frantic attempt to breathe...

Apparently Andrew Borden decided he was going to end the argument and the use of Frank's Box once and for all.

We don't sleep at the Lizzie Borden House anymore.

Foreword

My wife and I own the Mason House Inn in Bentonsport, Iowa. The Mason House was built as a steamboat hotel in 1846, the same year Iowa became a state. It was built for Billy Robinson, who called it the Ashland House. In 1857, he sold the hotel to Lewis and Nancy Mason, who renamed it the Phoenix Hotel. During the Civil War, the hotel was used as a field hospital for wounded soldiers on each side, as well as an Underground Railroad site. The hotel remained in the Mason family until 1956, when the Redhead family purchased it and turned it into a bed and breakfast, which it remains to this day. The Redheads put the Inn on the National Historic Register as the Mason House Inn. In 1989, the Redheads sold the Inn to the McDermotts, who owned the Inn until my wife Joy and I bought it in 2001. In 2016, the Inn celebrated its 170th birthday!

As soon as we moved in with our three children, we became aware of strange activity. We accepted the continuous sounds, movements, and tricks, but in order to try to understand them, Joy started a journal (*Joy's Journal*) documenting our experiences as well as our guests' experiences. This is now a three-volume set of books, with the fourth to soon follow.

Every spring, we offer tours to schoolchildren studying the Civil War, pioneer days, and the Underground Railroad. Joy and I dress up like Nancy and Lewis Mason and try to bring the house to life for the school children. In May of 2004, during one of these tours, a teacher took a picture of her class in Room 6. When they looked at the picture back at school, they were surprised to see the apparition of a Civil War solder in uniform sitting behind the school class. Up until this time, we did not talk publicly about the spirits at the Inn. However, this photo went through the small community like wildfire. Children brought their parents to the front door wanting pictures with the Civil War soldier... we had to tell them it doesn't work that way. Suddenly, we were on the map as a haunted hotel and our world quickly changed. For the next year, I looked at the photo and asked, "Who are you? Why are you here? Why did you show yourself?"

In February 2005, we received a call from Christopher Moon. He had heard about us from one of our guests, who'd had an experience at the Inn and was from Denver, where Chris also lived. The guest suggested that Chris might be interested in coming to do an investigation of the Inn.

We told Chris we already knew the Inn was haunted, that we did not want to go public with it, and we were not interested in him coming to do an investigation. We quickly learned that

Chris is a very determined man. He called us every week for the next three months. (We learned later that Paulette told Chris to "quit calling those poor people.")

Finally, Chris said the magic words: "I can tell you who is there and why." I immediately invited him for a visit, as I really wanted to know who the Civil War soldier was. So, in May 2005, we arranged for Chris to come and complete a two-day class and investigation. Chris planned to arrive Friday evening so he could do an initial investigation of the Inn. Unfortunately, due to car problems and getting lost, Chris and his father, Dennis, arrived at midnight. Having never seen a photo of Chris, we were a little taken aback when we met him at his car. Here was a long-haired individual with facial hair, standing next to his car. The first words out of his mouth were, "This place is humming." We immediately welcomed them in.

Chris and Dennis quickly pulled out all kinds of equipment and journeyed from room to room, from the basement to the third floor. Every place had strong readings, except for the formal parlor. We followed them around for three hours. Then Chris stated, "We now need to know who is here." And with the help of his father, he pulled a huge white "CPU" looking box from his car and placed it in the bay window of the dining room. He turned the box on, and everyone could clearly hear the white noise, as if between radio stations. Chris then directed us to ask the questions we had on our minds. He would tell us what was being said as we went along. In a short period of time, we had talked to many spirits, including Billy Robinson, Markie (the Civil War soldier), and a girl (Amanda) who played tea parties with our eleven-year-old daughter. I was not able to hear the voices very well at first due to the hearing loss I'd suffered in the Air Force. Fortunately I heard more and more as the session continued. Most of what we had initially asked was from the historical research we had discovered about the Inn and town of Bentonsport, Iowa, and was on our Inn's website.

After a while, I looked at Joy and said we needed to ask questions about things we had not yet published. My initial thought was that Chris had a cohort somewhere in town on a ham radio and the box in front of us was another ham radio (I have a science background) and the answers were coming off our website. After asking some key questions and getting the correct answers, the box made quick believers of us. More than a year after this event, Joy and I told Chris about our ham radio theory and he was amazed. In return, he told us we were the third location in the world where the box was used. (I thought it had been used for years and that our Inn was just another site.)

During the first year of investigations at the Inn, we turned on the Ghost Box after the class investigation was over. We sat in the dining room and held private discussions to help us gain more history of the Inn. Soon we discovered that class members wanted to hear this strange box and were more interested in this than the Electronic Voice Phenomena (EVP) that we did in class. So, we asked Chris to include the Ghost Box in every investigation, which he did. Chris and his family will start their twelfth year in 2016, with more than 1,300 individuals participating in the classes. Our spirits love Chris and want to share knowledge about their side. It is truly a lab for Chris and it is his most-visited site in the world. We consider Chris and his family part of our family, as we do the Inn's spirits. Thanks to Chris, Paulette, Dennis, and their fabulous Ghost Box, we have a better understanding of the identity of the spirits of the Inn and why they are here.

~Chuck and Joy Hanson

Introduction

This is the story of my quest to uncover the mysteries of the spirit realm. I want to know all of the details of the unseen world: what it looks like, what it sounds like, who inhabits it, and what we need to do *here* to reach it once our physical bodies no longer serve us.

I have been investigating and researching the astral realm for more than 35 years. My mom, Paulette, who is psychic, has been an invaluable partner in this endeavor. My dad, Dennis, is a skeptic, but he has been involved and helpful, in his own way, including being a partner of *Haunted Times Magazine*, the second periodical I published for many years.

Once I started conducting paranormal investigations full time, my focus quickly became two-way spirit communication. I tried all sorts of techniques in an attempt to speak with the other side. But it wasn't until I met Frank Sumption, the eccentric genius who invented the infamous Frank's Box or Ghost

Box (with a little help from engineers in the spirit realm) that I was able to really, truly communicate with spirits and other astral world inhabitants—including entities as diverse as ETs and Shadow People.

Frank's Box and Thomas Edison

Frank's Box is the completed version of Thomas Edison's infamous Telephone to the Dead. The device was completed in 2002 by Frank Sumption, a shortwave radio and electronics buff. As far as I know, I was the first person to ever use Frank's Box in an actual paranormal investigation. That was in 2003. The machine facilitates real-time, two-way communication with the spirit world and, as soon as my dad and I experienced it in action, we knew it would revolutionize the paranormal investigation field. The device requires mediumship ability on the part of the operator, not only to assist in translation but also to power the machine. The assistance of a Spirit Technician is also mandatory for safe communication.

Spirit Technicians

The idea of spirit technicians has fascinated me since I made first contact. It seems these individuals are from all corners of the universe. I believe Spirit Technicians are sometimes spirits that once lived on Earth in a physical body and sometimes—more often, actually—they are entities that did not exist on the earth plane or in any other physical reality. In my years of research, I found many of the Spirit Technicians were what you might consider extraterrestrial spirit entities. I believe that the

ET techs are more common due to their access to infinite levels of intelligent existence.

According to Thomas Edison via my communications with him, all of the individual beings that serve as Spirit Technicians were hand selected to work on this particular project and have been in place for some time. The Technician, not being a physical entity, has the ability to seek out and interact with specific spirits.

It's absolutely vital to work with a Spirit Technician when using the Ghost Box. The Spirit Technician is the gatekeeper who ensures not only that we are communicating with the specific spirits whom we're attempting to reach, but also makes certain that any negative energy is held at bay. I've had many experiences throughout the years in which dark entities have attempted to trick me into thinking that I was communicating with the spirit in need, when in fact I was being duped by a dark energy. I've learned to always listen to my Technicians as they tell me they "see things from the top of the mountain that I couldn't possibly see from where I stand." Many times the Technicians have drained the batteries in the device to stop these communications when I insisted on pushing forward. In one particular case, they actually physically flipped the device's power switch to the off position, effectively ending the contact.

Role of the Spirit Technician

The role of the Spirit Technician is a varied one. In the majority of my communications with Spirit Technicians, they've mainly been facilitators. I am aware there are different levels to the team that Mr. Edison assembled and I'm sure that I haven't communicated with all of them.

When I turn on the Ghost Box, the first thing I say is "Technicians, assist." I then ask for the name of the specific technician who will be assisting for that particular session. Once I have verified the name of the technician, I wait for a very specific sound to come through the speakers behind their announcement. This is my confirmation that the tech helping from the spirit side is a technician who works in the light. After that verification has been made, then—and only then—I will proceed with the session.

When I'm doing a private session for an individual, I ask my client to state their full name out loud and allow the technician to identify their energy. I wait for confirmation from the spirit tech that they have properly identified the physical person with whom I'm working. Once we have completed the introduction process, I ask my client for the full name of the person they are attempting to communicate with on the other side. I wait for the technician to let me know that they've identified the energy of the spirit with whom my client wants to communicate. A few technicians have told me that it's like identifying DNA when attempting to seek out a specific spirit on their side. When the technician acknowledges that we've reached the spirit sought, I encourage my client to say a simple hello and wait for a verbal response. It's usually only a matter of moments before we hear the voice of the client's loved one come through the speakers of the Ghost Box.

Spirit Technician Communication

I've been blessed to deal with scores of Spirit Technicians throughout the years. When I first communicated, it was very chaotic. I would say "Technicians, assist" and it sounded like a large group of people talking to one another and attempting to push their way through. After I heard a distinct voice, I asked, "Who am I speaking to?" After a brief pause, one of the entities would answer in a clear voice over the static and I would know that was the Tech who would be assisting me for that session.

Over time, things got more organized and I became familiar with a small group of spirits. After reaching this stage, I was fortunate enough to begin dealing with Technicians on a one-on-one basis.

Many of the technicians I've dealt with have spoken to me in clear English, which is by far the easiest way for me to understand and relay messages. I've also dealt with several different dialects, which seem to have either a Spanish or Italian origin. Some of the most intriguing dialects I've dealt with have been not of this world at all. Often when the entities that work as Technicians on the other side speak to me in English, it's very apparent the information is being translated either by another Technician or some sort of translation program. It's extremely hard to describe. The way I interpret it is similar to a computer or robotic voice coming through the speakers. In other rare instances, I've heard something I'd never heard before come through the device and for some reason I'm able to understand it, communicate with it, and relay messages. This is where my mediumship abilities prove invaluable.

Also—and I know this is an unpopular opinion for many researchers and psychics—there are very few people that were meant to work with these devices. It takes a very unique mediumship ability to not only receive messages from the device but also to power the device. The medium becomes one with the machine and the energy flows in a circular motion.

I've never had what would be considered a "bad" experience with the Spirit Technician—but there have been many instances in the past where I found it extremely difficult to work with certain Technicians, much like any workplace. Once I realize that my energy is connecting with one of these Technicians at the start of a session, I try to be as polite as possible and let the Technician know that I would prefer to work with another individual in the future. So far I haven't had any negative repercussions from doing this.

Spirit Technicians as Troubleshooters

I have many spirits that stay with the Ghost Box until they get their message through. I am always willing to help in the spirit of the light, but if they are disrespectful or pushy, I will ask my Technician to remove them from communication. From what I understand, they do so by simply blocking the bothersome entity from the device.

People have asked me if the spirits or entities stay in the device or if they ever come through in dreams, show up at my house, etc. In most cases, the spirits that attempt to communicate with me through the device will follow the device until it's turned on again. In the ground rules that I've set up, I insist that spirits speak only to me through the device. If they choose to harass me in an attempt to get their story through, I will simply ask a Technician to eliminate them from further communication.

Frank's Box Evolution

There were at least six incarnations of Frank's Box, each an improvement over the previous model—smaller, or with less static. The last version Frank Sumption was working on when he passed away even had a video component.

The first device Frank built was a huge, heavy machine that was extremely difficult to transport and required electricity to function. The second-generation device was about half the size of the first, much lighter, and included a handle for somewhat easier transport. The third-generation device was much smaller and ran on a large surplus of AA batteries. The only drawback of the third-generation device was that, due to the size of the machine, the speaker and power amps were much smaller and it was somewhat difficult to hear.

As for the fourth-generation Ghost Box, I contacted Frank with a specific request for a machine. The Spirit Technicians had come to me over several different sessions and told me what I would need for clearer communication. I contacted Frank and provided him with $275 to complete the machine to the Technician's specifications. Once again, without fail, Frank contacted me less than two weeks later with the completed device. It was a wooden box with a brass handle. There was a small latch on the front of the device and when you lifted the cover, the facing of the device was inside. There were speakers on the front as well as the sides of the device. It offered both linear and random function as well as an AM/FM source switch. The device had several different knobs for volume and rate adjustment as well as two antennas that ran from the upper left-hand corner of the device. This device, unlike the others, ran on rechargeable gel cell batteries. The machine could run for several hours without having to be charged again and offered the opportunity to use the machine in new and exciting ways. This is still the primary device that I use today.

Thomas Edison

Thomas Edison seems to be the brains behind this operation, which really is the embodiment of his "Telephone to the Dead." He's very much in charge and only comes through when a strong message needs to be delivered from up top. Rarely does Mr. Edison make an appearance during a private or public session, but when he does his voice is very clear and distinct as if he's achieved a certain spiritual level that I can't fathom.

I believe that my involvement with Mr. Edison's team was foretold long before I became aware that I would be involved in this project. I think the timing of the message "Technicians, assist" at the infamous Sallie House in Atchison, Kansas, was simply my introduction to the spirit team. I can't say for sure how many levels of the spirit team exist. It seems that Mr. Edison carefully thought out this project and I believe that he himself is being directed from a much higher level.

In a related case of synchronicity, during one of my Ghost Hunter University events I taught at the Mason House Inn, I discussed the Ghost Box and how Mr. Edison was the original inventor. An older gentleman's hand popped up in the audience who provided some insight on Thomas Edison. He informed me the way Edison used to work was by giving specific tasks to each person on the team. Each of these individuals was highly skilled in one narrow area of expertise. In doing this, Edison would be provided the highest level of quality and would ensure that no two individuals shared information with one another. This is the way he kept anyone from stealing his work before it was patented. Apparently, he called these individuals "useful idiots." I realized that, in a very strange way, I'm just another one of his useful idiots.

Purpose of Frank's Box

A few years after I started working with the Ghost Box, I had a very interesting discussion with Mr. Edison and a few higher-level members of his team about the wider scope of the entire project. I was told about a project code-named "The 2012 Directive." I was informed the veil between the worlds is thinning due to several different circumstances. Apparently, this had been foretold near the beginning of the project. I was told that my specific role was to take these machines into the world and expose as many individuals as possible to the realities of spirit communication and the messages that wait for them in the next world.

I wasn't sure what to make of this message at first. (Anyone who knows me knows that I check my sanity each and every day!) The thing that really amazes me is that everything I was told during that session has come to fruition. I was told I would be presented opportunities to share my gifts and the team's message, even in times when that seemed impossible. I've been amazed at the synchronicity that has occurred in my life since working with the Ghost Box—I seem to be put in the right situation at the right time, every time. Even in the instances I've questioned why I'm at a particular event with low attendance or a non-receptive audience, I have always been rewarded with being able to dramatically help at least one person.

I was also told there would be a large contingent that would attempt to discredit me and would work tirelessly to destroy my messages of enlightenment and hope. This was evident right from the beginning. I was told I would suffer immensely throughout these trials, and this, too, was a sad reality. But the message that resonated with me was that I truly had a team behind me and that if I stayed true to the message and the cause, we would overcome and thousands of people would be provided true comfort and hope through demonstrations of the device. This, too, has become a powerful reality.

I was conducting one of my college lecture tours and had been away from home for many weeks. I was doing a session at one of the schools and jokingly said out loud, "I wonder if I'll ever get a break?" And the voice from the box responded immediately, saying, "We have a desk here waiting for you." I knew at that moment that my work wouldn't end after death.

Frank Sumption

After Frank Sumption passed away in 2014, I wasn't sure if we would ever hear from him again. By then, Frank and his wife, Norma, had become good friends with my wife and me. In later years, Frank had become so despondent about individuals taking the work he had devoted his life to and trying to make it their own that he once publicly made the statement, "When I die, you'll never hear me come through one of my own boxes!" I'd always known that Frank was feisty and a little bit stubborn, so I wasn't sure if he would make good on that promise or not. I hoped he might see things differently when he crossed over to the other side.

Before I attended and spoke at Frank's funeral, I decided to turn on one of his boxes to see if he might make an appearance. I was delighted when he did come through and passed on some messages for his widow, Norma. I was also amazed when Frank made an appearance during one of my private sessions on his Video Box 1, which is like FaceTime with those in the spirit world. I immediately knew it was Frank when he showed up on the screen wearing his famous baseball hat.

Some time went by before I heard Frank's voice again, but he did finally make an appearance during one of my public sessions. When Frank's voice came through the Ghost Box, it was stronger than in the initial session I had with him. He seemed to have found his place on the team. I quickly learned that Frank had no intention of working as a Spirit Technician in the sense of becoming a facilitator of communication. Just as he was when he lived here on earth, Frank was mainly concerned with improving the technology, now from the spirit side of things, and taking advantage of the position that he had in the spirit world. It was good to get affirmation that our personality doesn't change when we cross over.

CHAPTER · ONE

Frank Sumption and Edison's Telephone to the Dead

In 2002, I was searching for EVP specialists on Yahoo groups to help me decipher Direct Electronic Response EVP, or DER EVP. I was well known in the paranormal community for being able to come up with new and unique ways to record ghost voices and communicate with spirits. (My role as co-founder and editor of *Ghost Hunter* magazine, plus years of conducting EVP sessions at paranormal investigations using a variety of original techniques, gave me a solid foundation of familiarity and expertise capturing and deciphering EVPs. This background, along with extensive experience in the field, had established my reputation as an EVP expert.)

My Yahoo posting read: "EVP specialists needed." I then went on to describe the position. Several people contacted me whom I hired, some that I still work with to this very day. The one email that stood out the most was from a guy named Frank

Sumption. Frank took the heading of the email and changed it to "EVP specialists?" He then erased the body of the ad and replaced it with a tirade of insults toward me. He basically told me I was a moron and didn't understand anything about spirit communication. I took offense to this email and wrote him back a scathing message. Thus began an epic flame war. For three solid months we wrote inflammatory messages to one another, never making any progress in our feud. One day, my mother saw me responding to one of these emails. Aware of my fight with Frank, she said, "It's time to end this."

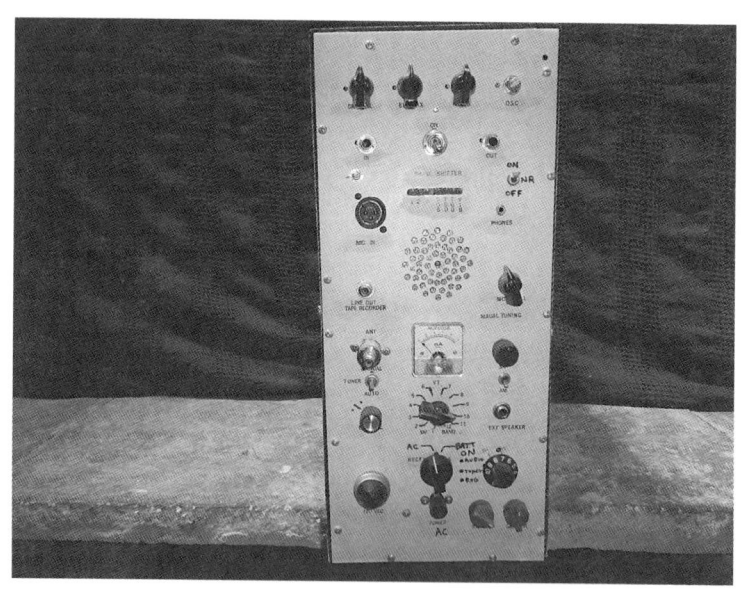

The first ever Frank's Box used in the field.

I wrote Frank back one last email that stated, "You stay on your side of the street and I'll stay on mine."

Frank replied with one last email, because that's just how Frank was. In the message he said, "You may wonder why I'm such an expert in EVP. I've completed Thomas Edison's Telephone to the Dead."

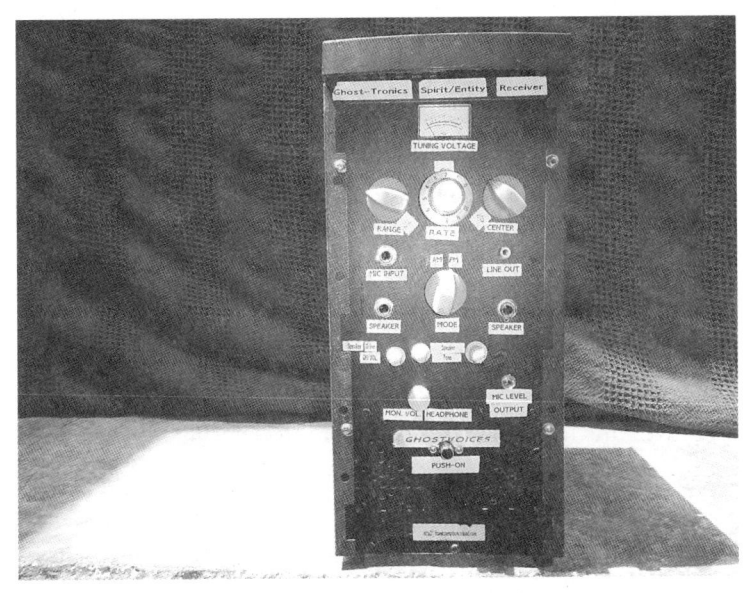

The second version of Frank's Box.

I laughed. *Thomas Edison's Telephone to the Dead? That was just a legend.* Researchers did know that it was a fact that Edison had begun work on such a machine. It seems crazy to think about an inventor with such an incredible scientific mind working on such a device. Apparently, Edison's mother was a Spiritualist and he was very close to her. After her death, Edison started to re-examine his views on the afterlife. He realized that since energy could neither be created nor destroyed and that it could only change form, we humans (being energy) had to go *somewhere*. Edison believed that he could create a machine that would not only bring through the spirit voices of people who had died, but also their personalities. He began work on the project and talked about his progress in publications such as *Scientific American* and *Forbes*.

His contemporaries were not at all happy with him publicly talking about this project. Upon his death, no machine or blueprints were ever found for the device. Those who know of Edison's work know that he kept meticulous notes about all of his ideas and everything that he worked on. Mysteriously, all of the pages regarding the machine that he was working on were torn out of his journals. It is commonly believed that his contemporaries, fearing Edison would be considered insane, tore out all of these journal pages and destroyed them. It is said that in the years following his death, Edison attempted to communicate with several mediums in an effort to complete the machine he had been unable to finish himself. Unfortunately, none of the mediums he contacted had the technical ability to begin work on any device. And so it became legend.

An early echo box built by Frank.

When I read Frank's claim that he had completed Thomas Edison's Telephone to the Dead, I genuinely thought he was out of his mind.

I wrote him back and said, "If you really completed Edison's machine, I will fly to any location you are just to see this thing work one time." It turns out Frank Sumption lived about fifteen minutes from my office! (You've got to love the Internet.) I set up a formal meeting with Frank, and the only logical place to meet was at the International House of Pancakes. My father and I dressed professionally, got our laptops and briefcases together, and went to meet Frank. When we arrived at IHOP, there stood a man looking *not* the way I had expected. He wasn't as tall as I envisioned and his long red hair was tied back into a ponytail under a tattered baseball cap. He wore a button-down flannel shirt with jeans and tennis shoes. I remember Frank looking back and forth at my father and me. Once he was convinced that we weren't CIA, NSA, or any other government agency, he decided he could tell us the story of how the machine came to be.

My father and I sat on the opposite side of the booth from Frank and his wife. He told us the most amazing story I've ever heard. Apparently, Frank was a shortwave radio buff who also liked to work with electronics at home. He was reading an article in a 1997 issue of *Popular Science* that talked about how one could hear "voices of the dead" coming through shortwave radio by conducting a certain type of experiment. Frank, thinking that there was a logical explanation for this, conducted the experiment to the article's specifications, with the intention of writing a letter to the magazine to debunk the claim. The first time Frank tried, voices came through shortwave calling him by his full name. Frank shut off the radio and walked away from it for several months. Curiosity got the best of him and he went back to see what else he could hear. This time, the voices not only called him by name but also told him how to complete Edison's Telephone to the Dead. The voices talked about circuit boards, diodes, and components.

Frank, being somewhat eccentric, listened to these voices and built the machine to their specifications. He said the first time he was about to turn on the device, he didn't believe there was any way it would work. While plans were simple, some things just didn't make sense. He flipped on the machine the first time and apparently those same voices came through the speaker much clearer than on the shortwave radio. They told him how to build a better device. Now, at this point, you have to imagine what my father and I were thinking. We had been kicking each other underneath the table almost the entire time Frank was telling the story in an attempt to not burst out laughing.

The third version of Frank's Box.

I said, "Wow, Frank. That is an amazing story. Is there any way we could see the device work sometime?"

He said, "Yeah, come down to my workshop next weekend and I'll show you how it works." The following Saturday came and my father and I arrived at his home. Frank's workshop was in his basement. As we began to traverse the stairs, I started feeling uneasy. The only way I can describe what I saw was a cross between a bad 1950s sci-fi movie and *Deliverance*. There were speakers hanging from the walls, there were wires hanging, there were fur pelts, and there were crossbows. As we walked into the main room, just to add a final perfect detail to the odd, ominous vibe of the room, there was a gigantic tinfoil pyramid hanging from the center of the ceiling. I turned to my father and whispered, "We're not going to make it out alive."

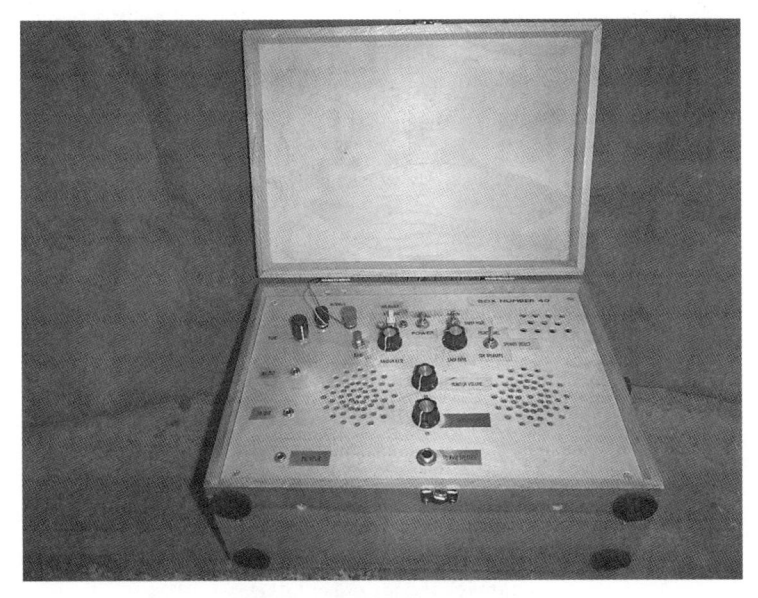

The fifth version of Frank's Box that Frank built to Chris's exact specifications.

When we first walked into that room, I saw, out of the corner of my eye, a huge 1980s-era beige computer tower on the workbench. It appeared that someone had ripped off the faceplate and shoved in gobs of wires and then made their own misshapen faceplate and screwed it on the front. It looked like there were several homemade switches and knobs on the front as well as handwritten labels done in marker. On top of the tower there was a small wooden speaker. As I took a few steps in the room I thought to myself, "Oh God, please tell me that's not it."

"This is it!" Frank exclaimed. I felt as if someone had drained me of all my enthusiasm. "Do you want to hear it work?" Frank asked excitedly.

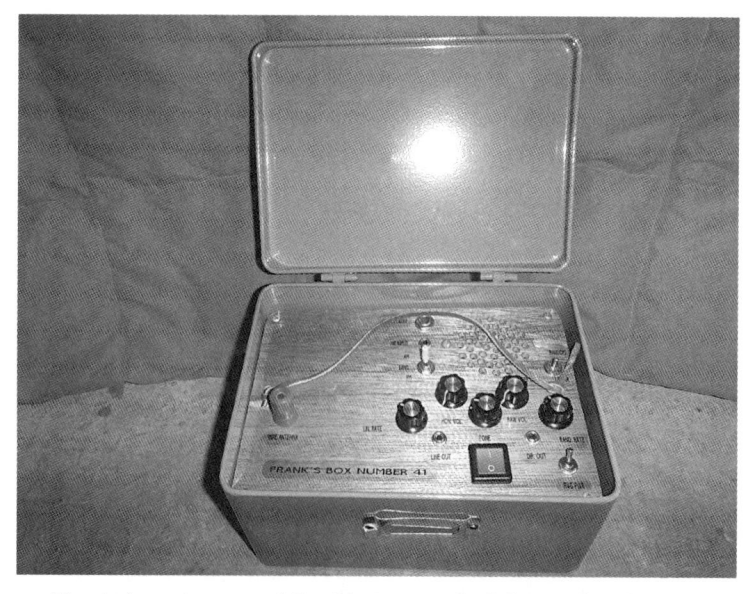

The sixth version, named Sarah's Box, was built by Frank and created for Chris's daughter Sarah, who has the same ability to hear spirits through the box as her father.

I took a few steps toward him and the machine and said in a doubtful voice, "I guess." Frank walked over to the machine and aggressively flipped a large silver switch on the front of the panel that was labeled "on" and "off" in magic marker. Several of the lights on the machine lit up and through the wooden speaker on top it began to make a strange "warm-up" sound. Suddenly, the speaker came to life, spitting out what sounded like static and random words. I could clearly hear snippets of local radio broadcasts in all of the confusion. It quickly dawned on me that this man had built a broken radio and claimed to be speaking to ghosts and aliens through it. I knew it was time to go. I looked at my father and he looked back at me and, without saying a word, we knew what the other was thinking. Nervous, I took a few steps backward, as did my father.

I told Frank, "Thanks so much for inviting us out here today, we really appreciate it." As I turned my back to leave I said, "We'll try to do an article on this in the magazine and see where it goes from there."

As my father and I started walking toward the door, we heard Frank yell, "Wait!" We both froze in our tracks. I slowly turned around to face Frank and as I did he said, "The voices said that you're supposed to take this with you."

I thought to myself, *the voices*. Instinctively, I started to reach into my back pocket for my wallet and in an extremely hesitant voice asked Frank, "How much does someone pay you for something like this?"

"You don't get it, do you?"

In a shaky voice, I answered, "No."

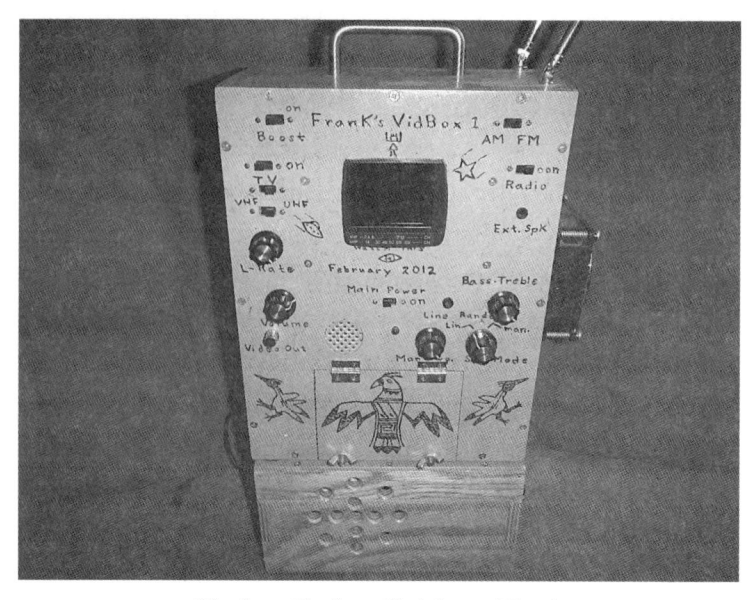

*The first video box. Chris bugged Frank
for a long time to create the first video box.*

Chris's echo box that was built by Andre.

There was a moment of silence before Frank stated, "I'm supposed to stay here and build these things; you're supposed to take this out and talk to ghosts." It felt like we stood there staring at Frank forever. Eventually my father and I moved at almost the same moment to break the tension. I grabbed one half of the gigantic machine and my father grabbed the other half. We didn't exchange many pleasantries with Frank after that as we quickly made our way up the stairs. As we left the house, both of us felt extremely on edge. We were driving an old white Jeep Cherokee at the time and I remember lifting up the tailgate and not gently setting, but rather almost tossing the device in the back of the vehicle. As we quickly drove away, it felt as though we'd survived a near-death experience. Both of us laughed nervously and recounting some of the strange details of what had just taken place. Suddenly, something dawned on me. *Frank and I had engaged in a huge flame war for several months, and he seemed to be some sort of electronics genius. What if he didn't build a Telephone to the Dead at all? What if he built some kind of dirty bomb and we were driving away with it?* I could visualize Frank standing in his driveway as we sped off into the distance holding some sort of remote control and muttering to himself, "Telephone to the Dead, my ass!"—then pushing the button and witnessing our demise.

But, we didn't blow up. Instead, my dad and I took the machine back to our office and stuck it on a shelf by the entrance. It sat on the shelf, unused, for nearly a year. We thought there was nothing to it whatsoever. When we walked into the office and saw it, we would chuckle. It became our "pick me up" for the day before we started work.

The holiday season arrived and we were preparing to shut down the office for several days. We had a huge investigation set up at the Sallie House in Atchison, Kansas, for just after Christmas. This was going to be a big investigation because it was our fourth time there and we felt we had a great chance at solving the crime that surrounded the house. I remember walking into the office that morning and seeing Frank's machine sitting on that shelf, dusty and unused. I thought to myself, "I'm going to prove to that guy that this thing doesn't work at all."

I got one of my digital voice recorders, plugged in the machine, flipped the big silver switch on the front, and once again witnessed the strange sounds coming out of the speaker on top. I set my digital recorder next to the speaker and walked away for the rest of the day. When I wrapped up my final emails of the day, I walked back over to the machine and shut it off. I grabbed my digital recorder and took it over to the computer where we did the majority of our EVP analysis. I plugged in the patch cord from the recorder to the computer and patiently waited for the large file to download.

When the notification popped up on the screen, I immediately plugged in my 1970s "Princess Leia" headphones and slipped them over my ears. As I pushed the play button, the sound that came through was just like what we had heard in Frank's basement—like a broken radio, basically—but louder. I tried to concentrate for quite a while, just to make sure I wasn't missing anything, but eventually my thoughts wandered to the upcoming investigation. I thought about the house, the town of Atchison, the spirits that we had already contacted, the poor little girl who had died there, and the mystery that surrounded the property. After some time passed, I realized I still had this annoying sound torturing my eardrums. I grabbed the mouse and prepared to turn it off. Just as I was getting ready to right-click, I heard something that took my breath away. A male voice said, "Your trip to Atchison." I froze. The sounds continued in my ear for quite some time before I found the sense to push the stop button. I rewound, eventually finding the spot in the recording I was looking for. Once again it said, "Your trip to Atchison."

It was at that moment I was convinced I had lost my mind. I started to listen beyond that point and could make out clear voices in the recording, stating facts that only my team and I knew. I had to quickly bring in a witness to make sure I wasn't losing my grip on reality. I called my mother and she came down to meet me. I started to play her snippets of things that I found on the recording and she was as stunned as I was. As I let the recording play, she heard something and her face turned white as a ghost. "Wait! Play that back!" After rewinding, you could hear another male voice saying two words: "Ice boat."

You see, my mother has always had dreams about being on the *Titanic* and has had a very clear waking nightmare of being in the freezing water as the ship went down, attempting to hold two blond-haired children's heads above the water. This was a distinct message to her. At this point, I wanted to make sure that we weren't just "hearing things," so I sent the recording off to one of my best EVP analysts. I didn't tell him what the recording was, I just asked him to see if he could find anything meaningful in it. He found more than twenty clear statements in that one recording. Like it or not, we had to test this device in the field.

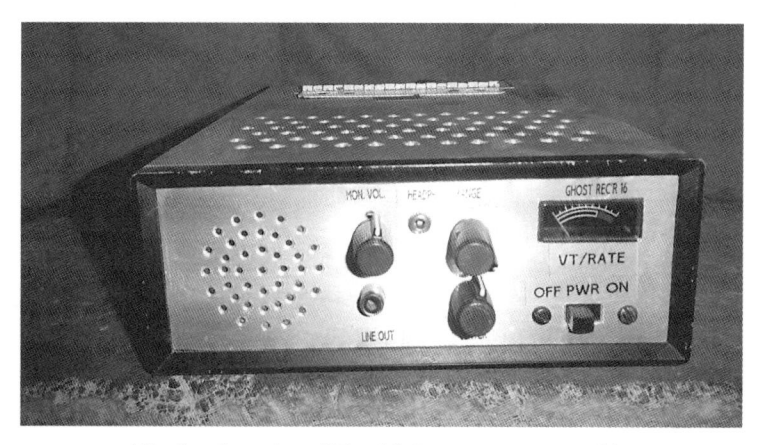

*The fourth version of Frank's Box was more portable.
It was the first to run on batteries.*

The second ghost box that was built by Andre.

We made the decision there was no better place on earth than Sallie's House to find out if this truly was the completed version of Thomas Edison's Telephone to the Dead. In a way we were right, since the spirit of Sallie, the innocent child spirit, did have something to say. We even thought we might hear from the man responsible for the child's death (a doctor)—and we did.

What we *didn't* expect to encounter was the doctor's inhuman astral world guardian.

CHAPTER · TWO

Sallie House

Not long after the oversized and under-appreciated "Telephone to the Dead" spoke to us for the first time, we left for Atchison, Ghost Box in tow. (Our investigation of the Sallie House using Frank's Box was actually our *fourth* investigation of the Sallie House property.) I should probably start at the beginning...

I was first introduced to the story of the Sallie House through the television show *Sightings,* which aired in the 1990s. It focused on paranormal activity and explored everything from ghost stories to UFO investigations. I remember being particularly fascinated by the story of a young couple that had moved into a small house in Atchison, Kansas, with their newborn child. Apparently from the moment they moved in, strange things began to happen.

At first it was small things, like items being misplaced, but it quickly escalated. The woman who lived there said she used to put the child to bed at the same time every night. One day, her next-door neighbors saw her outside and asked her why, each night after she put the baby to bed in the nursery, she would turn the light back on only a few minutes later. The neighbor asked if everything was all right. The woman explained that she seldom went back in the room unless the child was crying and that she rarely turned on the light. But the neighbor reiterated that the light came back on every night—they could see it from their room!

This obviously concerned the homeowner, who thought she might be having electrical issues in the house. The owners had the wiring checked and were told that it was old, but in decent shape. From there, things seemed to spiral out of control. The woman said she walked into the nursery one day to find a mobile above her baby's bed spinning wildly. Even stranger, all of the baby's stuffed animals were arranged in a perfect circle in the center of the room. Obviously someone had deliberately placed the toys in a circle, but neither she nor her husband had done it and the baby was too young to do so.

Frightened and curious as to what was happening, the woman began to snap photographs throughout the house. She was shocked when she saw strange mists, lights, and figures in the photographs. She had the film and camera checked out to make sure there was nothing wrong with them, and was told there were no problems with either. As the occurrences became more frequent inside the house, she feared for her family's safety.

She contacted the *Sightings* television show, asking them to come out and help her with her possible paranormal problem. After reviewing the evidence, the show's producers agreed to come out and investigate. They set up their base camp across the street at the Glick Mansion and went over every day in an attempt to record any strange occurrences. The crew was frustrated by the lack of evidence inside the house. They went to tell the woman they hadn't discovered much and, more than likely, would not be airing the episode. As they broke the news to the woman and her husband, the couple was clearly disappointed.

Suddenly, the man began to act very strange. He winced and hunched over in obvious pain. Startled, the crew asked him if he was all right. The man clenched his teeth and exclaimed, "She always does this when she gets angry!" He raised his shirt to expose his chest. To the crew's astonishment, they noticed small red marks begin to develop at the top of his chest and move down toward his abdomen. Very quickly the marks became deeper and clearer. Eventually blood began to drip from these scratches.

The shocked crew asked, "How often does this happen?"

The man replied, "Whenever she gets angry." The *Sightings* team was obviously fascinated by this new development, as it was something they had never seen before. They set up experiments in which they had the man sit in a chair in the center of the room and wait for something to happen. According to the show, they had several encounters with an entity that scratched the man repeatedly. They filmed the majority of these attacks.

Also, while these experiments were taking place, there was a bizarre incident with a rose. At one point, while the team was attempting to communicate with the spirit inside the house, they smelled something burning. When they went to investigate, they found that a single rose inside the house had caught fire with no apparent cause—it was still smoking when they found it. Mystified by this activity, the producers called in a famous television psychic to attempt to shed some light on why this might be happening. The psychic came to the Sallie House and did a full investigation. He later revealed his findings.

He claimed the house was haunted by the spirit of a seven-year-old girl named Sallie. According to his visions and impressions, in the 1800s, the house used to be a doctor's home. Sallie's mother had brought her daughter to this house in the middle of the night. Sallie had been complaining about severe pain in her stomach and her mother felt her ailment couldn't wait till morning. For some reason, the doctor decided to perform the exam in the upstairs bedroom, rather than in his standard medical room downstairs. He made Sallie's mother wait outside. Within minutes, he stepped out of the room and told the mother that Sallie was suffering from acute appendicitis and he had to operate right away or the appendix could burst and Sallie could die. According to the psychic's impressions, the doctor returned to the room, closed the door behind him, and attempted to give the child ether to sedate her prior to the operation. But when the doctor began to make an incision to remove the girl's appendix, the child sat up screaming! He hadn't given Sallie enough ether. In a split-second decision, he decided to continue with the surgery, even with the child wide awake. Sallie screamed and kicked while he attempted to remove her appendix.

The psychic said the last thing Sallie saw was the doctor standing above her with a sharp scalpel and bloodied hands as she faded off into death. He claimed that it was the little girl's spirit that remained in this house and who was responsible for all of the paranormal activity. The psychic also stated that the reason the man of the house was being scratched was because of Sallie's anger toward the doctor who botched the surgery and killed her.

After the footage aired, it became *Sightings'* highest-rated episode. They went on to film eleven additional episodes about the house, showing more fascinating footage each time. The family was finally frightened out of the home by the entity on Halloween night approximately one year later, and they swore to never return to the house. Allegedly, an older seductress spirit began to influence the husband and posed a physical danger to the wife and child.

While I was fascinated with the incredible story and the footage I saw on television, I was absolutely convinced it was fake. I was sure this was just "Hollywood magic" and they had created this story strictly for ratings. It wasn't until I was invited out to the Sallie House many years later that I was able to investigate for myself.

Sallie House—First Investigation

My first investigation of the Sallie House happened many years after I saw the Sallie House episodes on *Sightings*. It began when I received a call from the Atchison, Kansas, Travel and Tourism Bureau. They told me they were interested in promoting their haunted trolley tour during the Halloween season and asked if I'd be interested in coming out to investigate a few of their more well-known haunted houses. In negotiations with the man from the tourism bureau, I told him my team would definitely be interested in coming out, but that the infamous

Sallie House had to be included in the investigations. He told me that he would need to contact the owner of the property and get permission and that he would try to get back to me later that day.

After hanging up the phone, I enthusiastically called my partner at *Ghost Hunter* magazine and told him about the possibility of investigating the Sallie House. He was just as excited as me, and we discussed our views of the footage that we both hadn't seen for years. Around three o'clock that afternoon I received a call from the man from the tourism board letting me know we had approval to go into several of the houses in town, including the Sallie House. I was ecstatic at the news and started preparing right away. We decided this would be a great opportunity for our new intern to come along and write his nonbiased experiences, since he knew nothing about the Sallie House.

A few weeks passed before we made the long journey to Atchison, Kansas. We decided to drive the nine hours through eastern Colorado and Kansas as we weren't being paid for our time. We drove all day, maneuvering some pretty spooky fog-covered roads. It was nighttime when we finally arrived in the small town. The elderly couple that owned the Glick Mansion bed and breakfast worked with the town and agreed to let us stay at their beautiful B&B for free. We decided since we had a long day ahead of us, we would all go to sleep right away. I remember lying in my bed thinking about the day ahead. While I didn't really know what to expect, I was excited about the possibilities.

While we were having breakfast at the Glick the next morning, my contact from the Travel and Tourism Bureau arrived. He was a slender man with short hair and glasses and I could immediately tell he had no true interest in what we were doing, but was a good soldier and knew he had to deal with these "ghost people" to get the information and publicity needed to promote their tours. We shook hands and had a brief meeting about what was in store for us that day. He had a very precise schedule with a list of the houses we could investigate and specific times that we had to be in and out. We gathered our gear and followed him to the first location. Many of the houses we visited that day were occupied. The homeowners were very hospitable and we captured lots of amazing evidence inside their homes. My partner and I immediately began to comment about the extraordinary amount of paranormal evidence we were collecting in every location we visited. This town was definitely a hot spot, but we were baffled as to why.

One of my favorite investigations that day had to be at the McInteer Mansion. It was an extraordinarily large house that looked like something you would see in the movie *Psycho*, the finest type of Victorian building you could possibly imagine. I clearly remember how I felt as I stepped in the back door. I knew immediately that several of the former tenants were still there. Every room held some sort of evidence, whether it was EVPs or pictures of orbs and shadows. The current owner told us the macabre story of the elderly woman who died in her rocking chair inside the house during the summer. Apparently she had dozens of cats. When she died, none of the windows in the house were open and there was no air conditioning. The cats, unable to escape the house and with no food or water, soon turned their attention to the decaying corpse sitting in the corner of the mansion. Yes, they actually ate their former owner and it was several weeks before the townspeople could figure out where the horrific stench was coming from. When they finally realized what had happened, the smell was so bad that it had permeated all of the carpet and even the walls inside the home. Not only did all of the carpet have to be removed and replaced, but all of the floorboards in the house had to be covered in plastic as the stench had penetrated the wood. At this point I was absolutely sure the elderly woman's spirit was still inside the house looking for a way out, so before we left I made sure to address her by name and tell her that it was okay to move to the light.

We had a quick dinner that night, but all of our attention was focused on the highlight of our visit: our investigation of the Sallie House. Joining us was a newspaper reporter from the town as well as a cameraman from a local Topeka television station. The Travel and Tourism Bureau had released a press release about us coming to town and doing an investigation of the Sallie House and the media didn't want to miss out on the chance to grab a piece of evidence or at least a good story. Our guide told us that it was going to be a cold night, as the Sallie House was under renovation and there was no carpet or heat inside the house. When I pressed our guide as to what happened in the home, the only information I could drag out of him was that the last tenant, a woman, practiced some kind of dark magic. She hadn't paid her rent for several months and when the owner of the house pushed to have her removed from the property, he was horrified to find that the house was in complete and utter disrepair. He reported that all of the carpets had been covered in fecal matter and that the woman had made a makeshift satanic altar in the basement, including an inverted pentagram with animal sacrifice remains still sitting on and around it. Our guide ended his statement with a nervous laugh as he looked toward the floor. I looked at my partner and our intern with concern.

When we finally arrived at the house, I was a little stunned. I didn't realize that it was directly across the street from the bed and breakfast where we were staying. Though it was fairly cold outside, there were several townspeople milling around, obviously interested in our investigation. We pulled up to the front and got out. When I looked up at the small structure, my stomach turned. It was a modest white home—but the second story window immediately drew my attention. The three of us didn't speak as we pulled equipment out of the vehicle. I internally struggled between what I was experiencing on a psychic level and my perceptions of everything I'd seen on television. It was much more difficult than I could have possibly imagined. It was apparent to me that our guide wanted to get this portion of our visit over with as quickly as possible. Before we had taken all of our equipment out of the car, he had already made his way up the path and onto the porch and was attempting to open the door.

Equipment in hand, we made our way toward the house to meet up with our guide, the newspaper reporter, and the cameraman. Our guide was fighting the lock on the door, furiously jiggling the keys. Finally, as if someone had unlocked the door from the other side, he pushed the door open. He nervously walked through the front door and began fumbling for light switches. When several lights flicked on, I could see there was a staircase directly in front of us, and a room to the right. We all walked in hesitantly and I remember the piercing energy and bizarre smell of the house. While it was cold outside, it felt like something was causing it to be even more frigid within the house. My legs felt weak upon entering and I experienced a buzzing inside my head. I was extremely confused by the energy, as it was nothing I had ever felt before.

When I walked into the room on the right, I felt sadness surrounding me. Looking around at the other people who were there, I believe they felt it too, whether they acknowledged it or not. We had to be careful where we walked and set things down, since there was no carpet but there were exposed carpet tacks everywhere. Once our equipment was settled, we began pulling out as many handheld tools as possible. During all of this, I was drawn upstairs by something or someone. As I began to ascend the stairs, I immediately noted the feeling of sinking into the floor, as if the wood were quicksand.

When we reached the landing, two rooms stood out to me. In front of me, just off to my left, was a room that emanated a strange combination of energies. As the cameraman filmed and the reporter jotted down notes, our guide told me, "This was the nursery. I guess quite a bit of activity happened in here." I cautiously entered the room and was amazed by the contradictory energy of something extremely strong and evil and something shy and innocent. I began to snap pictures inside the room and caught several spirit orbs on my digital camera. I turned to show my results to my partner, our intern, and everyone else in the room. Everyone gathered around the small viewfinder to see the results. My partner was taking pictures and videotaping and getting similar evidence.

After spending a few minutes in that room, we turned our attention to the second room that had drawn me in. As I took my first step in, our guide said, "This was the doctor's bedroom and it's also apparently where the little girl died." Before he had even spoken the words, I already knew exactly where I was. Quick flash images from long ago filled my mind. I could still sense the fear, anger, and hostility that were imprinted in that room. For some reason I was drawn to the dressing closet and this is where we decided to do our first EVP session. We gathered in a circle and started to ask questions into the open air. My partner and I were on the same page on how to attempt to communicate with this little girl. We both spoke to her as you would speak to any seven-year-old child. We asked her if she was there, if she would talk to us, if she was scared, and if she needed our help. We were shocked when we actually heard a few audible voices and whispers inside the closet while we did the session.

After we wrapped up the recording, we went downstairs to investigate a bit more. When we got back to the first level, we went to the kitchen for the first time. While the rest of the house was painted white, the kitchen had one dark red accent wall that drew my attention, though at the time I couldn't figure out why. I noticed the door to the basement was open. We flipped on the light and went down to the narrow basement space. It was partially finished with concrete, though a good section of it was still dirt. It looked as if someone had knocked out a portion of a false wall made of brick. The remnants of the black-magic pentagram were still on the floor and, needless to say, it made me extremely uncomfortable to be anywhere in the vicinity of it. Our companions on this investigation were becoming antsy as they started to feel an unnatural coldness settle over the room. We were all capturing anomalous images and sounds on our equipment. We returned to the first floor to discuss what we would do next. Our guide asked, "Okay, are you ready to get out of here?" He'd had more than enough paranormal exploration for one day.

I was ready to review our evidence to see if we could prove or disprove the Sallie story when something spoke to me on a psychic level. I can't say I consciously meant for the words to come out, but they did. I said, "Let's get out of here. There's obviously nothing going on inside this house. It was all a hoax." My business partner looked at me as if I'd lost my mind. I gave him a knowing wink and he nodded and said, "Yeah, I agree. This place is a total joke." We then motioned to everyone to leave the house. Our guide, completely confused by what was going on, was just happy we were leaving. Upon exiting the house, we saw that several more townspeople had gathered on the other side of the street waiting for something to happen. Our team marched across the street back to the Glick Mansion and met inside the parlor. We quickly pulled out laptops in an attempt to review what we obtained. As the downloads began, I told everyone in the room, "We're going back in there." Everyone but my partner, who immediately understood my reasoning, looked at each other with confusion.

The newspaper reporter asked, "What do you mean? Back to the Sallie House?"

I said, "Yes. There were several spirits hiding that didn't want us there." While I was discussing my impressions of what was going on inside the house, my partner had downloaded the audio and played back several intriguing voices, including that of a little girl who was obviously reaching out to us. At this point, the newspaper reporter had experienced enough and decided to leave. We thanked her for coming and gathered the remaining part of our team, which included our reluctant tour guide and our very brave cameraman.

My plan was simple. Though I don't believe in antagonizing a spirit in most cases, I knew we needed to burst into the location to draw out the negativity that was present. We gathered up a few handheld investigation tools, including still cameras, video cameras, EMF meters, and a white noise machine. The five of us quickly jogged across the street and opened the door as fast as possible. We burst into the house, yelling and screaming, in an attempt to shock the negative spirits that I believed were hiding. We flashed cameras, turned on noisy meters and white noise machines, and asked questions to the open air. Everyone there felt immediate tension inside the small house. I could clearly see that our intern was very uncomfortable with what we were doing and our tour guide was caught somewhere between feeling silly about what he was doing and scared of what might happen. I was drawn to the kitchen again and the odd red wall. I pulled out my Trifield Natural EMF meter and began scanning that area. The readings were off the chart, and without any mundane explanation, I began to consider the possibility of that area being a vortex. As I got readings, my partner snapped pictures and recorded video. He said he was capturing quite a bit of energy. I said, "I think this might be a vortex."

At that moment, I felt excruciating pain at the top of my head, as if someone had taken a nail and hammered it into the top of my skull. I dropped the meter and hunched over in pain, grabbing the top of my head. My partner, shocked, said, "What's wrong?" I told him what I experienced and he began to pull my hair apart to see if there was anything there. The cameraman was filming the entire time. In the spot where it felt like a nail had been pounded into my skull, a large red welt was beginning to form. I was stunned and dizzy and there was consensus in the room that it was time we left.

I said, "No. We need to find out why she's doing this." While everyone was recording, I pulled out my voice recorder and began to pose questions to the little girl's spirit. I said, "Sallie, why would you do this to me?" I tried to leave time for her to reply, but in my confused state, I was asking rapid-fire questions. A minute or two into my interrogation of this poor little girl's spirit, something came to me on a psychic level. At that point I said, "Wait a minute, this isn't Sallie at all. You're the doctor! You're the one who's doing this. Why would you do this? Who are you trying to protect?"

The instant I called out to the doctor, one of the most frightening things that has ever happened to me occurred. It felt as if someone had taken a hot clothes iron and stuck it to the side of my face. I could feel the burn start at the top of my left earlobe and go all the way down my neck to my shoulder. The cameraman gasped—he could see the heat coming off the side of my face. This was the first time I was ever attacked by a spirit. I immediately realized there was no way to fight something that wasn't on our dimensional level. I couldn't hit it; I couldn't run away. I just had to wait for it to stop.

I yelled into the room, "Why are you doing this?" The response was immediate and hostile—it felt like something reached up through the floorboards into my legs and pulled all of the energy out of my body. As I began to fall to the ground, my partner grabbed me and pulled me toward the door. Everyone present understood the severity of the situation and what they were witnessing and quickly attempted to get out of the house. In recalling the situation afterward, it was like experiencing missing time, with disjointed scenes flashing before my eyes. I remember getting out of the house and cold air stinging my skin. I remember all of the lights being turned off in the house and the door being slammed and locked. I remember concerned townspeople asking what happened and my partner rushing past them. I also remember looking back into the dark house that suddenly looked as if someone had turned a massive television on inside. I saw flashing white lights in the windows of the Sallie House and I knew nothing natural was causing it.

When they finally got me back inside the Glick Mansion, the innkeepers told me I needed to get to a doctor, as they could clearly see the burn on the side of my face. I was in shock and only wanted to recount everything that happened to me with the team. The proprietor handed me a glass of aged whiskey and told me to drink it. I took a few sips before realizing I needed to sleep. The minute my head hit the pillow, I was out. When I woke in the morning I wondered if the entire experience had all been a dream. When I got up and started to get ready for the day, I looked at my face in the mirror and saw the burn had all but disappeared. I then realized that the spirit had used my own energy to create the burn. I knew then that this would not be my last visit to the Sallie House.

Upon returning home from the Sallie House the first time, I began to feel as if I hadn't left all the house's negative energy in Atchison. My wife mentioned she was seeing things out of the corner of her eye. I didn't want to cause panic so I told her that I believed the experience had left both of us shaken, though I felt there might possibly have been something attached to one or both of us.

Sounds of knocking from the ceiling, walls, and rooms became an everyday occurrence. One night when I was alone, I decided to pull out my digital camera to take some pictures around the house just to see if there was anything there. To my astonishment, orbs filled every room in our house and the majority seemed to be focused in our family room. I felt it was important to share this information with my wife, so I ended up showing her the pictures. This did absolutely nothing to calm the situation.

It wasn't until a few days later that my wife, daughter, and I were watching TV in the family room when we heard one of the most frightening sounds I have ever heard. My daughter and I were on a couch that sat up against the wall and my wife was sitting in a chair across the room. I noticed my young daughter becoming emotional and suddenly scared. The hair stood up on my arms and a knot formed in my stomach. It felt as though something massive was hovering over our backs. Instinctively I looked over my shoulder and grabbed my daughter to hold her close. At that moment, we all heard the unmistakeable sound of dogs viciously fighting emanating from the wall behind us. I pulled my daughter from the couch and moved her across the room. All three of us clearly heard the terrifying dogfight racket and stared at one another in disbelief.

Once I snapped out of it, I threw open the sliding glass door and ran through the yard and around the house to see what was causing the sound. When I reached the far side of the house, there was absolutely nothing there. I placed my hands on the seven-foot fence and pulled myself up to look over the top to see if there was anything in the neighbor's yard. Once again there was nothing.

I stood there for several minutes contemplating what to do next and tried to pull myself together before reporting the news to my family. My daughter, being extraordinarily savvy when it comes to the paranormal, immediately knew that something was drastically wrong. We made a decision as a family to do a clearing in the house. The next night when I was alone in the house, I decided to burn sage and fill the house with white light and positive energy. Once the ritual was complete we never heard from that particular entity again.

Sallie House—2nd and 3rd Investigations

From my very first investigation at the Sallie House, I knew this property wasn't going to be like any other property or type of investigation I had been involved with before. When my partner from *Ghost Hunter* magazine and I planned our second investigation of the Sallie House property, we decided we wanted to get to know some of the townspeople in the hope they might be able to give us insight into the house and hauntings.

While we did conduct investigations inside the property on the second visit, the majority of evidence came together through research at the library. We were able to take information gathered during electronic voice phenomena sessions and use it to compare with physical records. To our astonishment, almost everything added up. When we finally wrapped up that investigation, the former tenant provided us with some detailed accounts to take with us and help us prepare for our third investigation.

Nearly six months passed before I returned to the Sallie House for the third investigation. That time, I made the decision to bring my mother with me, hoping she would experience the energy and be able to give us insight into the haunting with her psychic ability. It didn't hurt that she was also a great researcher—I knew this would be a benefit. Our third visit to Atchison was during the winter and the owner of the property had done some work to make it a little bit more livable. We stayed across the street at the Glick Mansion with the innkeepers who had now become friends. We spent a full day investigating the Sallie House while collecting some amazing evidence. Several of the townspeople, including staff at the library, met with us to relate stories they had heard about the house through the years. The library staff was also able to research and dig up some new information that helped us in the investigation.

We traveled throughout the town gathering information and talking to individuals who had heard stories passed down from older relatives. We were able to document Sallie's last name as Hall and actually found her in the census records during that time. We also discovered she was at least part African-American. When we went to the town cemetery to look for a grave, we were disgusted to find they had paved over the section where Sallie's grave was reported to have been. The African-American population at that time was so disrespected that they were given small plots where they would actually bury one family member on top of the next. When it came time to put the new road in, the city decided it wasn't worth it to move the gravestones or graves. In addition, a very dark and seedy underbelly to the Atchison, Kansas, of the late 1800s was becoming evident. The crime, depravity, and money lust of the era seemed to create a deep evil in the very heart of the town.

Through tireless research in the three-day investigation, we were able to locate Sallie Hall's birth and death record as well as her family's census records. I still remember the shock and elation that we felt when we found out, via census records, that Sallie actually existed and that she was of both African American and Caucasian descent.

While Atchison, Kansas, is well known as the birthplace of Amelia Earhart, the famous pilot, there is no way that we could have known that she wrote a journal entry regarding the spirit of the little girl on Second Street. This was great validation that even during Amelia Earhart's childhood, the spirit of Sallie Hall was well known by the locals.

While we left our third Sallie House investigation with more questions than answers, it felt as if a major breakthrough was about to happen.

Sallie House—4th Investigation

Now we were going back to this very haunted property with Frank's Box, which seemed, incredibly, to be working, therefore presenting us with the perfect opportunity to hear what happened straight from the spirits of those involved. Since this was our first time using the device, and to our knowledge, the very first time it had ever been used in any paranormal investigation, we were excited and curious to see how Edison's Telephone to the Dead performed in the field, rather than in a lab setting.

As we drove eastbound on I-70, my mother, father, and I tried to come up with the best game plan to use the device during the investigation. We were supposed to arrive sometime in the early afternoon, so we decided we would take the machine up to the most active room in the house (which was the nursery), get it set up, turn it on, and then leave for the day. We'd then return with our whole team that night to see if anything came through the Ghost Box. It seemed like a solid plan at the time. We weren't, however, counting on having car trouble.

When we finally arrived in Atchison, it was very late in the afternoon. We quickly unloaded our suitcases into the Glick Mansion. Then we drove to the Sallie House to unload all of our equipment, since the amount and size of the equipment required us to drive the short distance.

When we arrived, my father and I jumped out of the Jeep and started to pull gear out of the back. I noticed my mother was staying firmly planted in the front passenger seat of the Jeep. I set down a large speaker and walked to her side of the vehicle. I asked her, "Are you ready? Are you coming in?"

She said, "No way!" I realized the sun was starting to go down. One thing I had learned from investigating the Sallie House three times before is that this wasn't a property you wanted to go into alone or with fewer than five people—it was far too active and truly dangerous. I laughed a little bit with my mom to ease the situation and told her I understood.

My father and I decided the best thing to do was to take just Frank's Box up to the nursery, get it set up, and then get out fast. I remember the feeling of sadness and of being watched by invisible eyes as we walked in the front door. We hurried up the stairs to the nursery and started putting the machine together. Once it was assembled, I plugged the power cord into the wall and flipped on the power switch in the front. The device started to make its typical warm-up noise and then emitted some broken radio sounds. We started to gather our things to leave. It was at that point that something hit me—I realized no one had ever used this machine in the field before and I should probably say something. I held up my finger as if to say, "Just a minute," to my father and had an idiot moment. I stood in front of the machine and said in a shaky, almost childlike voice, "Um, if there are any ghosts in here who want to talk, please speak through this machine that Frank built. It's good. Um, I already heard things through it."

My extremely skeptical father stood there and looked at me as if I had completely lost my mind. I stood there staring at the machine when suddenly a phrase came into my mind and I blurted, "Technicians, assist." I had no idea who or what a Spirit Technician was at this point. I also had no idea where this information came from, and after I said it, I really felt confused about its source. I didn't give it much thought at the time, however, since I knew it wasn't a good idea for just my dad and I to be alone in the house and I was feeling a strong urge to leave. I looked at my father, he looked at me, and we made our way out of the room and started down the stairs. We made it about two steps down when, from behind us, we heard the sound of white noise blaring through the speaker on the machine. It sounded like someone had turned the volume all the way up. We both froze in our tracks. It felt like we stood there forever but in reality it was probably only thirty seconds.

Then we heard the voice of a male spirit say very clearly, "Sallie, listen." Every hair on my body stood on end and I hunched over, fingernails digging into the wood banister. I looked over at my father and he was frozen with shock as well. Then we heard one of the most amazing things I've ever heard, even to this day. The little girl's voice that we captured *dozens* of times on open air EVP came through the speaker of the Ghost Box. The male entity was attempting to train her on how to use the device effectively! We stood there and listened to the two spirits speak back and forth until it was pitch black inside the house.

We finally pried ourselves away and went back to the Jeep to get recording equipment in hopes of capturing some of this exchange. There sat my mother in the exact same spot we left her quite some time before. When we explained what was taking place, she looked at my father and me like we were absolutely crazy. We finally convinced her to venture into the house and she helped us bring the equipment up to the nursery. Once we had recorders and video cameras in place, we began to do question-and-answer sessions with the spirits. To my amazement, we found that when we asked questions into the open air, the spirits would reply in their own voices right then and there through the machine! This truly was the Telephone to the Dead!

At one point during this investigation, I was alone in the nursery. My parents were downstairs working on equipment issues. I was asking questions via Frank's Box in an attempt to understand what had caused the haunting. While trying to reach the little girl's spirit, I was contacted by the doctor who was responsible for Sallie's death. When I began to ask questions of the doctor, his voice came through the speaker very clearly. It was at this time that I learned via the Ghost Box that the doctor had a mistress. In addition to the doctor's voice, another more frightening voice was present. It could only be described as inhuman. When I pressed for answers, I was threatened with being scratched. When I continued with the interrogation, I clearly heard the sound of scratching coming through the vents in the room. I wrapped up the session but left the night vision camera running.

When my parents and I reviewed footage of the period after I had left the room, we found not only video evidence of spirit activity, but also a vocal exchange between the spirit of the doctor and the inhuman voice coming through the Ghost Box. The doctor stated, "You were supposed to protect us." The inhuman spirit responded with a blood-curdling roar. Upon hearing this, I felt a deep sickening shock run through my entire body. All at once, the true scope of the haunting became clear to me.

I believe that, after the doctor passed away, he returned to this house on Second Street in an attempt to keep the past and his crime buried forever. A scared and hateful man in life, he carried that same personality into purgatory. Through the emptiness and fear that plagued him in this new existence, I believe he unwillingly summoned demonic entities, which now possessed him in the middle ground. He worked with these dark forces in an attempt to protect his name and legacy. When we arrived with Frank's Box and were able to speak directly to the spirits involved, we became a true threat. What we heard on the recording from Frank's Box was the doctor communicating directly with demonic forces, informing them that they hadn't kept up their part of the bargain.

After hearing the doctor's angry outburst and the demonic roar, we placed the Ghost Box in the master bedroom upstairs, which was the room in which Sallie died. My father and I talked back and forth with the spirits in the room. We talked to the spirit of Sallie and told her that we cared about her and wanted her to go be with her family in Heaven. We warned the negative spirits that we wouldn't be bullied into leaving and told them that we would not bargain with the demonic. We attempted to speak to the doctor's mistress and told her that we knew it was she and the doctor attacking the living and then blaming it on Sallie.

The thing that was most amazing about using Frank's Box for the first time in the field was having the ability to communicate with spirits in their own voices and have them tell us things that we would have never known unless we'd spoken to them directly. We were able to take quite a bit of information the spirits gave us and actually document factual, historic events from their words.

For a long time it was thought that Sallie's spirit was the entity causing not only the physical scratching, but all of the paranormal activity in the house. When we were able to speak to her as well as the other entities, it became very clear that Sallie was simply a scapegoat for the attacks.

Speaking through the Ghost Box, the spirits made the shocking assertion that Sallie's father was the doctor, the man who killed her. (Though plausible, we have no way to verify this claim.) The spirit of Sallie's mother made another disturbing allegation via the Ghost Box: she stated the doctor's mistress not only pressured him into performing the botched operation that resulted in Sallie's death, but then remained with him inside the house even after her death.

It seems the mistress was responsible for the majority of the attacks on individuals who entered that house. It was stunning to hear her distinct accent; we believe it to be a Creole accent. She clearly admitted to several of the crimes and also seemed to claim she was responsible for sexually violating the man who lived in the house during the period of the initial attacks.

We were astounded with the results from the Ghost Box. The ability to directly communicate with spirits and hear their voices (or roars) in real time was something that was unheard of at that point. I suspected this would be a tool that we could utilize in all our future investigations. Even though there was quite a bit of static and delay with the first-generation machine, the potential of the device was evident. It was at the Sallie House, during our fourth investigation of the property, that we realized the field of paranormal investigation would never be the same again.

CHAPTER · THREE

Spooky Childhood and Haunted Times

People are always asking me how I became interested in ghosts and haunted houses. I think it's because of my haunted childhood and because my mom, Paulette Moon, can occasionally see spirits and ghosts.

I had a near-death experience (NDE) at around age two that I believe contributed to my psychic abilities and affinity with the spirit world. All I can remember prior to the NDE is that I was in a floating device in my grandparents' swimming pool. (I'm told that while the family was on the other side of the pool socializing, I floated some distance away from them and was splashing and playing. At some point the flotation device capsized and my entire head and upper body were submerged under water. It took quite a while before anyone noticed that I had flipped.)

My memory of the event was me desperately struggling to breathe before experiencing a sudden calm. As the strange calm soothed me, I felt myself begin to rise and I was soon looking down at my body and the entire scene from far above. I felt a comforting warmth as I ascended. Soon the only vision I had was of the brightest, almost white light calling me in. It felt very natural and I wasn't afraid. The next memory I have was being thrust back into my body as someone hit my back, desperately trying to revive me. I spit up quite a bit of water and then coughed uncontrollably.

I had the first paranormal experience that I can remember at age seven. (My mom remembers an earlier incident that involves me, which I'll share later in this chapter.) My family and I moved into a house in Englewood, Colorado. The house was built in the 1970s and didn't look scary or spooky, but from the moment I walked in, it felt different. It was summertime when we moved in and it had no air conditioning, so the first night we tried to sleep, we were hot. The house was on top of a hill and behind it was a large field that led to a creek bordered by a dense thicket of trees. Behind the creek was a restaurant and bar. I clearly remember lying in my bed tossing and turning, but all I could hear through my open window were the sounds of people laughing and talking and glasses clinking. Frustrated with the noise as well as the heat, I opened my eyes. I was shocked to see the silhouette of a little Indian boy standing at the end of my bed. For the rest of the night the spirit child never moved or said a word; he just stood and stared.

The spirit boy appeared nightly in my room for months. Whenever I saw him, I froze. For a long time, I was too scared to speak. When I finally mustered the courage to ask questions (from behind the covers)—questions such as: *Who are you? What is your name? Why are you here?*—the boy eventually dissipated. He never answered my questions or spoke at all.

The Indian boy played a huge role in my life, as he was the first ghost I saw. Seeing the spirit boy inspired me, at age seven, to someday become an amateur ghost hunter. It was also the catalyst for my life's mission to prove to my skeptical father that my encounter with the spirit world was real. (Although the spirit boy stopped coming around when I was sixteen, he apparently didn't leave—my daughter saw his image when I took her back to see the old house.)

We had other ghostly occurrences in this house as well: doors opening and closing of their own accord, strange shadows, and light anomalies. Objects disappeared and reappeared on a daily basis. For example, if someone left their car keys on the kitchen counter unattended and returned to get them later, they'd discover the keys were gone, having seemingly vanished into thin air. I remember many times tearing the house apart looking for things only to return later to find the missing object in the exact spot it had been set down.

One of the strangest paranormal experiences at our house was the night that ghostly sonnets played for hours on our family's 100-year-old baby grand piano. When my great-grandmother passed away, she willed a very old baby grand piano to my aunt. The problem was that my aunt was living in an apartment at the time and had no room to store it. Since we had a fairly large house, my mother agreed to keep the piano. The piano was delivered a week or two after my great-grandmother's passing. I was excited about having the piano in our house, as it was the first time I had an opportunity to teach myself to play. The piano was extremely large with a polished brown finish. It was in a state of disrepair; the keys were tarnished and worn.

I remember standing and staring at the huge old piano for some time, oddly intimidated. When I finally gathered up the courage to sit down on the bench, I reached up and gently pushed one of the higher keys. It made a strange creepy sound. I didn't know much about music at that time, but I knew this piano was definitely out of tune. That wasn't enough to stop me. I stepped on the pedals and experimented with the different keys up and down the board. Even though the piano was drastically out of tune, I started to make sense of how the tones worked together. I found several very old music books inside the bench and, one by one, I set them up on the stand over the keyboard and attempted to decipher the notes. (I never did learn how to read music, realizing I was fortunate to be born with a good ear and that it was easier for me to figure out songs on my own.) I played the piano until dinnertime that first night. I imagine I drove my parents crazy with the loud clanking sounds emanating throughout the house for hours.

That night when we went to sleep, I was genuinely excited about the possibility of being an accomplished musician in the future. I can't say that night felt any different than the other nights in the house when I closed my eyes to sleep. I had no idea my parents and I—yes, even my skeptical father—would experience a bout of paranormal activity in our living room that night.

I'd been sleeping for a few hours when I was awakened by the distinct sound of music coming from somewhere in the house. As I opened my eyes and attempted to understand what was happening, I realized I couldn't move. Within minutes I was fully awake and still completely paralyzed. The strangest thing was I didn't panic. The music I heard was beautiful. It sounded like a single piano being masterfully played and I can recall a strange sense of calm coming over me. I don't remember sleeping much that night, only dozing when I saw light coming through the blinds in my room.

When I woke up in the morning, I was more tired than I had ever been in my life. I got out of bed and slowly descended the stairs, rubbing my eyes and yawning as I made my way into the kitchen. My parents, who were sitting at the kitchen table, said, "Good morning."

My mom said, "You look exhausted!"

I told her I hadn't gotten any sleep at all with all the music playing. I'll never forget my mother's and father's response—my parents stared at each other in disbelief. Over breakfast, they shared their experience of the previous night. Apparently, both my parents were awakened by the sound of the music as well. They said that they, too, experienced the same paralysis I did. They also told me that both our cat and German shepherd raised their heads to listen, but neither animal got up to investigate the sound, which was odd, especially for our dog.

I could see my father was bothered by the incident but wouldn't acknowledge a ghostly explanation. He simply shrugged it off as a neighbor playing a radio too loudly. My mother and I looked at each other knowingly and shook our heads. It was obvious to me, and I believe to her as well, that it was my great-grandmother coming back and playing her old piano to let us know she was okay. Interestingly, when I was seventeen years old, I wrote a song on that old piano called "Goodbye." One day after school, I was working on the melody when my mother came into the room with a stunned look on her face. I stopped playing, looked back at her, and asked, "Are you okay?"

She replied, "Do you know what you're playing?"

I said, "Yeah, it's a new song I'm working on."

She said, "That's the song we heard that night at the old house." The realization that my mom was right hit me all at once. It was, in fact, the ghostly sonnet that my parents and I had heard so many years before.

In our family, we have a lot of unique characters. My mom has traced our genealogy and found out my great-great-grandfather was a Southern Cheyenne Indian chief. On my mom's side of the family, we discovered that our ancestors came from Saracena, Italy. Many people consider Saracena, not Sicily, to be the Mafia capital of the world. (There was a time that the Pope wouldn't even go there!) In addition, we are related to three Polish rabbis—I believe that's where the Kabbalah magic comes in. My great-great-great uncle was Queen Victoria's personal physician.

There was another psychically gifted group in our family: the Scotch-Irish side. My grandmother, great-grandmother, and great aunt had special abilities. My grandmother was a clairvoyant who was able to predict the future with amazing accuracy. My grandmother was able to read people's energies and could tell right off the bat whether or not a person was genuine.

My mom's great aunt Anna taught her to read fortune cards, which Mom later found out were a version of tarot. Whenever there was a problem in the family, Aunt Anna used to say to my mom, "Let's sit down and see what the cards have to say."

Through every card she flipped over, she gained insight into what was happening. It never failed to amaze Mom when Aunt Anna would check in with someone in the family and find out that she was spot-on in her predictions. Aunt Anna's abilities helped her in many different ways, including some that were considered "not quite" legal. It turned out she and her husband were bootleggers who specialized in bathtub gin and Chianti wine in their North Denver home in the late 1920s. When it was time to make a run to the local speakeasy, she would consult the cards to see if the speakeasy in question was law-enforcement free. She must've been pretty good because they were never caught.

My grandma was a woman with quite a few talents aside from her psychic abilities. During the 1940s, she was a big band singer featured in the Dave Munro Orchestra, which performed live radio broadcasts from well-known hotels and locations around the country. After her singing career, she went on to own several businesses and had a spectacular business mind. Unfortunately, later in life she started to show signs of Alzheimer's disease. After my grandfather unexpectedly passed away, it was quite clear Grandma wasn't the person she had once been. Even though she was stricken with this debilitating disease and its quick progression, she would suddenly snap into a coherent state and relay a vital psychic message to me. I attempted to understand as many of Grandma's message as possible and then, just as quickly as she was "back," she was gone again. I feel this shows just how strong my grandma's psychic ability was.

The 1950s Colorado my parents grew up in was extremely conservative. My mom's family absolutely did not want anyone to know about their psychic abilities for fear of ridicule. While my mom was in elementary school, she never shared with anyone that she was psychic. By the time she was in middle school, she decided to tell a few classmates about her unique abilities. Her friends would ask her questions like, "What's going to be on the algebra test?" or "Is there going to be a snow day so we don't have to study at all?" Those types of questions were innocent enough.

It wasn't until high school that she realized her abilities could get her into real trouble. Her girlfriends would ask, "Is my boyfriend cheating on me?" Regardless of the answer, she didn't want to say anything because she knew it was a lose-lose proposition. When finally pressured into answering, if she had news they didn't want to hear they would say, "Oh! Why would you tell me that?"

When my mom was a junior in high school, she met my dad. At the time, she didn't share her psychic abilities with him because his mother was a devout Catholic. My mom shares the time my dad called and told her he had to help his mother clean out the garage and that he would call her the next day. She saw very clearly this was not the case.

When he called her the following day, she asked him, "So, where were you really yesterday?" He stuttered and said, "I already told you; I was helping my mom clean out the garage!"

She said, "No, you weren't! You were at the Offbeat 3.2 Bar drinking beer and playing pool with your friends."

He replied, "How did you know? Who saw me?"

She told him, "Oh, it's just woman's intuition." And then she slammed her blue princess phone down in his ear.

A few years after my parents married, my mom discovered she was pregnant with me. She says she was overjoyed by this news; she couldn't wait to find out if I had her psychic abilities. Even before I was born, she wanted me to have a love of music so she put her stomach up to the stereo speaker and played classical music like Van Cliburn. She jokes that something must have gotten crossed in the wires because I prefer Van Halen to Van Cliburn.

No one wore seatbelts in their cars in those days (1973) and in fact, Mom says she doesn't remember if her 1973 red Camaro even *had* seatbelts. While driving one day, she was hit from behind at a fairly high speed. The doctors put her on immediate bed rest. She says it was one of the hardest things she's ever had to do.

While on bed rest, my mom had a mystical experience three months before I was born. She awoke one morning to see the full-bodied apparition of a woman standing at the edge of her bed. It didn't frighten her; as a matter of fact, she felt very comfortable. The woman didn't say a word, but communicated with her telepathically. The spirit woman's message was very clear; she insisted that if I were delivered by C-section, I would die. At that moment, my mom made the decision she would never allow that to happen.

Once the apparition's message was delivered, she simply faded away. When the experience was over, my mother wasn't sure what she was supposed to do with the information. Should she call her OB/GYN and tell him about the warning? She asked herself if this was something that happened to every pregnant woman or if it was unique to her. She decided not to say a word to anyone about the experience, fearful of what they might think.

When she went into labor, the warning was firmly in the back of her mind. There was difficulty right away and she experienced nearly twenty-four hours of back labor. The staff told her they were going to have to take me via C-section and, remembering the warning, she immediately began to panic. Most of the hospital staff became impatient with my mom's adamant objection to a C-section, but a nurse named Marianne respected her decision and decided to make one last attempt at a natural delivery. She came in the room and began to massage my mom's stomach and adjust me into a standard birthing position. I was born shortly thereafter, without any drama. My mom says she truly believes that if she hadn't heeded the warning, I would not be here today. When she glanced at the clock she saw that it was 3:16 am on March 25. It hit her that the grandmother she had lost five months earlier was born on March 24. It quickly dawned on my mom the apparition who passed along the warning was her own grandmother!

My mom's recollection of my near-drowning incident was that the adults had all gone for a swim in her parent's pool in Texas. They put me in a flotation device in the pool so that I could safely enjoy the water. Everyone was sitting around the pool having fun while I splashed in the water. Suddenly, they realized there were no splashing sounds coming from the pool, only silence. They looked and saw, to their horror, that I was completely submerged upside down in the flotation device, my feet flailing in the air. At first, everyone froze. Shock turned to full-fledged panic when my frantic feet suddenly stopped moving.

My aunt quickly swam over and flipped me right side up. I was motionless. My aunt pulled me out of the flotation device and swam to the side of the pool while everyone jumped into action. They rolled me on my side and attempted to get the water out of my lungs. Mom says it seemed like quite a bit of time went by, but they were all relieved when they heard me cough and saw water spill out of my mouth as I began to cry.

My mom finds it interesting that I have such a detailed memory of the event, which we later discovered was a true near-death experience. We believe this only enhanced my psychic ability.

As I previously stated, the first paranormal experience that I can recall happened in the house we moved into in Englewood, Colorado, but my mom clearly remembers my first ghost experience happening while we were still living in Colorado Springs, Colorado. While in school, I came down with a stomach bug and became very ill. I had a bunk bed at the time and liked to sleep on the top bunk. My stomach was extremely upset and my mom tells me I repeatedly climbed down the ladder, went to the restroom, and vomited. Each time she heard me get up, she got out of bed and came to my room to make sure I was okay before helping me back into bed. It was a long night and we were both very tired.

The next morning I was sitting in the kitchen, feeling better and eating breakfast. My mom says I asked her a very strange question: "How did you lift me back up into the bed so easily last night?"

My mom replied, "What do you mean? You climbed up the ladder by yourself the last time."

My mom says I told her she lifted me up and set me in the bed and then rubbed my head until I went to sleep. At first she thought I might have had a vivid dream, but when she asked me for details about the person who helped me into bed, she realized it was the same apparition that had warned her about my birth so many years earlier. It turns out my great-grandmother was still looking over us, making my mom extremely happy.

When we moved into the house in Englewood when I was seven years old, I began to have nightly spirit encounters. My mom decided it was time to find out if I had her psychic ability.

After listening to my accounts of strange things that were taking place in our house, my mom decided to start taking me to purportedly haunted locations throughout the Denver area. One of the first places she took me was the Molly Brown House during the week of Halloween. She thought this would be a safe environment for me to experience the house and hear other people's ghost stories. I was intrigued with not only the stories, but also the second floor of the house. My mom saw I was experiencing something, as I became very quiet, but I didn't say at the time what it was. Having a father who was a skeptic, I truly wanted to prove that I was experiencing something real.

After this, I became an amateur investigator and wanted to go to additional locations to understand what these energies and entities truly were. When I was thirteen or fourteen, we had the opportunity to go on the Capitol Hill Haunted Mansion Tour, which was held the month of October. This tour allowed participants to walk through some of the most haunted houses in the Capitol Hill neighborhood of Denver. My mom and I were familiar with some of the properties, since we had been to them before, but there were a couple of new houses on the tour that fascinated us.

The first house resembled a French castle and was called the Croke-Patterson-Campbell mansion. It looked like a true haunted house. We wandered through the halls of the large structure and it was clear there was paranormal activity inside. My mom saw from my focused expression that I was sensing all of the spirits present.

After touring the large property, we were guided to a carriage house on the side of the building. As we walked in, we could see they had transformed it into a modern office space with circular tables and signs in the entranceway. We made our way up a winding staircase into the upper portion of the building where volunteers from the historical society were giving a lecture. Wanting to listen from the beginning, we moved to the side wall away from the crowd in hopes of getting a good seat for the next lecture.

As we leaned against the wall, I started to gasp and flinch. My mom grabbed me by the shoulder and said, "What's going on?" I was grasping my neck and couldn't speak. I ran down the spiral staircase, stumbled toward the front door, and then out onto the lawn where I tried to catch my breath.

I told my mom, "Something was choking me in there!"

She asked, "Like someone had their hands around your neck?"

I said, "No, like I was being hung!"

After a few minutes, we decided to give it one more attempt and go back in the building. As we walked by the front desk, my mom asked the volunteer, "Can you tell us why my son had a choking sensation upstairs?"

The volunteer replied, "Oh, that's just Willie. He's a friendly ghost." My mom and I looked at each other in disbelief. When we returned upstairs, the room had cleared out and a new group was coming in to hear the lecture. My mom and I looked around to see if we could find anything that might have explained the choking. It wasn't until the volunteer started to tell the story of the Croke-Patterson-Campbell mansion that things became much clearer.

The speaker told us about a previous caretaker, known as Willie, and explained the connection with the movie *Poltergeist*. Apparently Willie was a Satanist. While he was the caretaker at the Croke-Patterson-Campbell mansion in the late 1800s, Willie began to do side work for the city of Denver. He was in charge of removing the bodies from the city cemetery and moving them to Mount Olivet and Fairmount Cemetery so they could use the vacated cemetery property as the new Cheesman Park. The problem was that Willie and his crew decided it would be easier to just move the headstones and leave the majority of the bodies in the park and no one would be the wiser. Even more disturbing was the fact that many of the exhumed bodies never arrived at their new resting places. Willie dug up the coffins and took them back to the carriage house via horse and wagon. Legend has it that he stacked coffins five high in the basement coal storage room. It is also said that Willie would use the bodies for ritualistic purposes.

As the story was being recounted, my mom and I felt extremely uncomfortable. The volunteer continued, explaining that Willie didn't limit his desecration to the remains of the dead, but, it seems, he would actually lure animals and small children in from the dirt road that ran in front of the house. The volunteer then pointed his finger toward the west-facing wall where my mom and I had originally stood inside the room and asked, "Do you all see that railroad tie hammered into the wall?"

My mom and I slowly turned our heads in the direction the man pointed. My mom's heart skipped a beat as she realized what the guide was going to say, a moment before he revealed the information. "That's where Willie hung the animals and children and performed rituals on them."

She immediately knew I had directly picked up on the energy of the terrified victims who hung underneath the railroad spike—that spot was precisely where I was standing when I experienced the choking sensation. The room where we were had twenty or so people standing and listening and it suddenly felt crowded and hard to breathe in, as if there was no escape. The guide continued, saying, "Willie got sloppy and was eventually caught and punished for what he had done. As a matter of fact, he was hanged right out front where he used to lure those poor souls in off the street."

The moment the presenter finished speaking, my mom and I looked at each other and then immediately focused on a small window at the top of the room facing onto the street. It had glass on the outside, a chain hanging on the inside, and another pane of glass on the interior. It was obvious to both of us there was a presence there at that moment. The chain inside the window began to slowly swing back and forth and quickly accelerated. My mom asked the guide, "Do you see the chain moving inside that window?"

He glanced over his shoulder. Stunned, he said, "Um, yes I do!" He continued on. "That's impossible, that glass is airtight. There is absolutely no way that chain should be moving." We knew that Willie was still there. While my mom had always wanted to see how I would interpret paranormal activity, she admitted she wasn't prepared for that.

Afterward, we stood in front of the carriage house trying to grasp what had just happened. When we felt we had balanced and centered our energy well enough, we decided to move on to the next house. While the Croke-Patterson-Campbell mansion was intimidating, the next house that we encountered—the Peabody Mansion—was simply sinister. Had we known how the Peabody and its malevolent cast of astral denizens would consume me for the next three decades, we never would have set foot inside. The Peabody Mansion story, too complex and encompassing to be contained in a single chapter, will be told in a future book.

CHAPTER · FOUR

Lizzie Borden House

Another notorious haunted property we investigated with a macabre and violent history is the Lizzie Borden House in Fall River, Massachusetts. My father and I were vendors at a paranormal conference held in Las Vegas, Nevada. You always meet interesting people at these events and this time was no different. While sitting at our booth selling our *Haunted Times Magazine,* we were approached by a young woman and an older-looking gentleman. They stood over us for a few moments before I looked up and engaged the woman's glance. She said, "Hello" and I simply replied, "Hi." She went on to tell us that she was the manager of the Lizzie Borden Bed and Breakfast Museum and asked if we would be interested in conducting one of our Ghost Hunter University events at the house. We were looking to expand into different markets and this seemed like a great way to get our name out on the East Coast. I accepted and said we would be in touch to set up details.

I'll be the first to admit I didn't know much about this location or its history. All I knew was the creepy nursery rhyme that went: "Lizzie Borden took an axe, and gave her mother forty whacks. When she saw what she had done, she gave her father forty-one." So I knew it was time to give my mom, the sleuth historian, a call to see if she could fill me in on the details. When I told her about the opportunity that we had to not only teach a class at the Lizzie Borden House, but also conduct a full-blown investigation, she was very excited. She told me about the terrible crime that had taken place at the house in the late 1800s. Apparently, it was the site of a legendary double homicide—an unsolved axe-murder. According to police reports, someone had attacked Lizzie Borden's stepmother with an axe in one of the upstairs bedrooms while she made the bed. The attacker then went on to brutally kill her father, Andrew Borden, with the same axe while he rested on the couch in the downstairs parlor. When interviewed, Lizzie claimed she was in the barn eating pears during the time of the attacks. She stated when she entered the house she discovered her father's body and in horror called to the maid who'd been washing windows outside, exclaiming, "Bridget, come quick! Someone has killed Father!"

At this point the police were called in, but they completely bumbled the investigation. Not only was the crime scene trampled through by dozens of people involved in the investigation, but the public was also allowed in to see the crime. Sensitive and crucial evidence was completely destroyed within minutes. Photography was still a very new technology, but they were able to bring in someone to shoot the crime scene photos, which, while grainy, are still some of the most disturbing images photographed to date. The maid and Lizzie were both interviewed, since they were the only people within the crime's vicinity. The police took what evidence they had, but weren't quite sure how to proceed with the investigation. They researched several people of interest, including relatives and business associates of Mr. Borden, but the trail quickly turned cold. It was quite well known that Andrew Borden was a shrewd businessman who wasn't afraid to step on toes to get what he wanted. He was also considered quite the miser. He had accumulated a great deal of wealth throughout his life but never seemed willing to spend it on anyone, including his family. At the time, things like indoor plumbing and refrigeration were becoming commonplace, especially for people of wealth. Andrew Borden would have none of that. He kept his family in what was considered an average house with no amenities. He even forced the family to eat spoiled meat to avoid waste.

Lizzie had a taste for a better life and pleaded with her father to move them to one of the mansions up on the hill, a much more prestigious neighborhood in their town of Fall River, Massachusetts, but her pleas fell on deaf ears. As the police narrowed down their list of suspects, they took into account Lizzie's hot and cold relationship with her father. The police kept an eye on the house night and day. On the night of the murders, the police saw something extremely disturbing—lights appeared in the basement and, as the police officers watched, Lizzie attempted to burn an article of clothing in the incinerator. When questioned about why she was burning the clothing, she stated she had gotten red paint on one of her dresses and it had to be destroyed. Things were quickly becoming clear to the police. When they conducted a second investigation of the basement, they found the head and partial handle of an axe in the dirt beneath the washbasin. They felt they had their smoking gun. Lizzie Borden was arrested and charged with the murders of her stepmother and father. She was held in prison for nearly a year while the highest profile trial in United States history took place in the small town of Fall River, Massachusetts. Lizzie's sister, who was out of town at the time of the murders, was her staunchest supporter, standing by her side throughout the legal battle. Lizzie maintained her innocence throughout the course of the trial and would regularly exhibit dramatic emotional swings. In the end, the jury of twelve men decided a female couldn't possibly have the strength or rage to carry out such a heinous crime, and Lizzie was acquitted of the murders.

Though she was exonerated by a jury of her peers, the townspeople gave her the verdict of guilty and whispered and shunned her everywhere she went, including church. She ended up buying a house on the hill as she had always wanted and went into seclusion. Lizzie and her sister had a sudden disagreement and went their separate ways, never to speak again. Lizzie lived out the rest of her life as a recluse, only associating with actors and actresses at get-togethers at her home. She never married and left her fortune to charity. On her deathbed, it is said she made a confession but the contents of that interaction were never disclosed. In the end, no one ever found out if Lizzie did it or who the true killer was. It was—and remains to this day—the oldest unsolved axe murder in American history.

I was completely fascinated by this account and looked forward to our event. A few weeks later, I contacted the manager of the bed and breakfast and we set a date for three months out. It seemed like an eternity for the day to arrive. When it did, my mom and I flew into Boston Logan Airport and rented a car. We had our arrival day to kill so we decided to drive to Salem, known for the famous witch trials, and conducted an investigation at the Hawthorne Hotel, which was known for its extremely high level of paranormal activity. We were given full access to the building and the marketing director accompanied us on our investigation. The evidence we collected was incredible, including a picture of ectoplasm in the shape of a child's foot. The marketing director invited us back to do a Ghost Hunter University event at her location in the near future.

The next day we made the very long drive to Fall River and, as odd luck would have it, just as we started out, a heavy snow began to fall. In the days before GPS units, we had to rely on a map, which wasn't helping much. It wasn't hard to find Fall River, but it was nearly impossible to find the famous Lizzie Borden House. We drove aimlessly through the snowy streets looking for anything that would point us in the right direction. At one point, lost in a residential area, we asked the postal carrier if he could tell us where the house was. Unfortunately, we still weren't accustomed to the heavy Massachusetts accent and became more lost from his directions. I can still remember the frustration we felt, knowing we had to find the house since our class was scheduled to start at 5:00 pm sharp. My mother and I were getting a bit testy with each other from the strain. Then, seemingly out of nowhere, we saw the sign for the house and with a sigh of relief, quickly pulled in.

The house was remarkably tall and, even though it was covered with snow, you could see the dark green paint peeking through. As we drove alongside the house, I thought it was interesting that there was a front door facing the street, but the side door with a porch looked more like the main entrance. Immediately in front of us, there was a smaller building that we later found out was the reconstructed barn that now served as a business office and gift shop for the manager and owner. We parked in the lot behind the house amongst a few cars that belonged to staff and individuals taking the museum tour.

We got out of the car and gathered our equipment. Because we were late, we knew we had to set up quickly. We tromped to the back porch and lifted our gear onto the landing. Knocking on the back door got no response, so I tested the doorknob and it opened. I gently opened the door and was immediately bombarded with a rush of toxic energy. The only way I can describe the feeling was being bowled over by some terrible virus that immediately left you weak in the knees and sick to your stomach. It was extremely hard to take the first step inside the door, but when I did, everything hit me all at once. My mother quickly followed and when I looked at her face, I knew she was experiencing something similar.

Before the two of us could discuss what was happening, the manager summoned us into the kitchen. We walked down the hallway, passing a staircase on our right, as well as a closed door. The hallway was tight and had a very claustrophobic feeling to it. When we walked into the kitchen, it felt like a large room even though it wasn't. The manager was there and welcomed us in before introducing us to her friend who was busily cooking. She explained we would have a small class that day. While I listened, I looked throughout the room, noting the skillful way they had made a modern kitchen look authentic to the time period of the murders. The manager asked if we would like a tour before the event and we accepted, but I explained we needed to set up our equipment first. She motioned us into a room off the kitchen where we would conduct our class. It was a small dining room and the projection screen we had requested wasn't there, so we had to improvise by putting up a white sheet on the wall for a presentation. While we were in the midst of setting up, I noticed several artifacts from the murders, including crime scene photos, newspaper articles, writings, and actual artifacts from the scene of the crime. I was fascinated how the energy imprinted itself inside the structure. I was well aware this crime had taken place more than 100 years earlier, but to me, it felt like it had just happened.

Once we were set up for class, we returned to the car to get our suitcases and find out where we would stay that night. The manager directed us up the staircase and said our room was on the second floor. We climbed the narrow, winding staircase up one level and entered the room she gave us. It was a large bedroom with what appeared to be a smaller bedroom connected on the far wall. I told my mother she could have the large room, taking the small room for myself. We put some of our things away before heading back down to meet the manager for our tour. We started back in the kitchen and then moved on to the dining room where we had set up for the class. She explained to us that it was the room the police used for the autopsies and that the bodies remained there for quite some time while the investigation took place.

At this point the reality of the situation dawned on me. We exited through a second door of the dining room into the parlor area with a couch resting against the wall. A Ouija board and books sat on another wall. Knowing the very real risks of using a Ouija board, especially in a place like this, I cringed. The manager explained this was a replica of the couch on which Andrew Borden had been murdered. She showed us how the attacker had approached and killed Mr. Borden, according to police calculations. She brought us into the front room where the interviews had originally taken place. It contained very pervasive, oppressive energy. Leaving the room, we walked into the front entryway, which was surprisingly small. We then followed her up the front hall staircase and I chuckled as I saw a sign halfway up the stairs that read something like, "We've already had two severe head injuries in this house; watch your head."

At the top of the stairs there was a bathroom off to the left. Directly in front of us was another room with an open door. As we walked in, I immediately noticed a mannequin with an ornate period dress and hat. The manager noticed my interest in the clothing and asked, "Did you ever see the Lizzie Borden movie that starred Elizabeth Montgomery?"

I said, "I don't think so."

She told us that was the dress Elizabeth Montgomery wore in the movie. I smiled at my mother and she smiled back, both of us recalling my childhood watching reruns of *Bewitched*.

The smile on my face quickly disappeared as I felt something ominous on the other side of the bed. I slowly walked through the room to get near the area where I felt the disturbance. As I got close, I felt lightheaded and experienced a severe pain in my temple, which caused me to grasp the side of my head. "What happened over here?" I asked. The manager grabbed a picture from a nearby dresser and handed it to me. It was the crime scene photo of Mrs. Borden, who was hunched over on her hands and knees, blood everywhere. I was standing in the exact spot her murder had taken place. It was like nothing I had ever experienced. It was as if I experienced some of the feelings she felt during the murder.

I couldn't figure out if this was a recording—a timestamp of sorts that I was experiencing—or if Mrs. Borden was consciously reaching out to me to try to explain what happened. My mother saw my expression and grabbed me by the arm and gently pulled me away from the spot, knowing things could quickly get worse. My mom had been experiencing so much empathic resonance I was surprised that she was able to continue on the tour.

As we left that bedroom, we turned to our left. I think I expected to see a hallway, yet we were immediately in another bedroom. Lizzie's room didn't emanate any true energy for me, but I could see my mother was experiencing quite a bit. While the manager was talking about the room, I was primarily interested in moving the tour along. We moved through Lizzie's sister's room without incident and ended up back in the room in which we were staying. Before the manager opened her mouth, I noticed a picture of Andrew Borden hanging on the wall. I realized that this was, in fact, his room. She explained that the room I was staying in was actually the dressing closet. It was impressive to think of anyone having a closet that large, especially at that time, considering it now held a large bed and furniture.

She took us up one more flight of stairs to the third floor where there was a series of smaller bedrooms. She explained this was where the maid, Bridget, lived at the time of the murders. She also said there was quite a bit of paranormal activity reported in this area from guests who stayed on this floor. Most of those reports had to do with the spirits of children running through the rooms, laughing and playing. It was interesting how different the third floor felt from the previous two floors, almost disconnected. By the time we descended the stairs, a small group of students were arriving and we knew we needed to begin our class.

As the attendees gathered and found seats in the room, I realized we hadn't seen the basement area, something I'd been drawn to since we walked in the house. It would have to wait until after class. Though a small group, everyone responded extremely well to my Ghost Hunting 101 class and asked several great questions. After the presentation, we had a small dinner where the group could talk to one another and ask my mother and I additional questions.

The attendees were then taken on the same tour we had taken earlier, but they were taken through the basement as well. We pulled out all of our equipment, which included cameras, EMF meters, voice recorders, and of course Frank's Box, which at this time was still one of the larger units. When the group returned to the kitchen, I asked them if they were ready to go on a ghost hunt of the Lizzie Borden House. Everyone was excited, including my mother and I. We felt that with our equipment and expertise, especially the Ghost Box, we could get some genuine answers to what had taken place there unlike any investigator before us, paranormal or otherwise. Though the house wasn't large, we really hadn't planned where to start our investigation. So we decided to do an open-air EVP session in the parlor where Andrew Borden was murdered.

We tested the room for EMF spikes, and found several that weren't made by natural causes. (EMF spikes have always been associated with paranormal activity, so many investigators believe that spirit energy carries high levels of EMF.) We were also encouraged by the photographs we had taken, seeing quite a bit of orb energy in the room. We were able to document orb movement on the night vision video camera as well. We conducted an EVP session where each attendee had a chance to ask a question to the spirits of the house. Upon reviewing a few minutes later, we were all surprised at the level of spirit interaction on our recording. We had captured everything from an elusive Class A EVP to DER EVP as well. The group was revved up by our evidence.

We decided to go to the room where Mrs. Borden had been killed for the next portion of our investigation. Of the ten people in our group, I asked for three volunteers to stay outside while the rest of us went in. I did a short presentation on residual energy and how it could affect us in the physical plane. I asked the group to not say anything as I brought in one volunteer at a time. I led each individual to the spot where Mrs. Borden was killed and asked them to close their eyes, relax, and let their bodies do whatever came to them. I stood behind them as they closed their eyes and each time, one by one, they started to wobble back and forth before eventually falling either backward or forward. As I caught them and they opened their eyes, they were completely stunned by the experience. I explained the residual energy that was still present in that spot and how they were becoming part of what had taken place, experiencing something similar to what Mrs. Borden had. It was an incredible opportunity and a great teaching tool.

We walked through more rooms, obtaining readings and taking pictures with many great results, but no matter what I did, I was focused on going to the basement to conduct a Frank's Box session. After finalizing an investigation on the third floor, I told the group we were heading down to the basement to have a two-way communication with the spirits that remained in the house. There was a deafening silence at first, and then a nervous buzz that traveled throughout the group. We descended the stairs, all the way down to the back hall, where we walked towards the kitchen but stopped at the door just before we entered.

This was the entrance to the basement. The light was already on in the hall, but it didn't seem to do much to illuminate the rickety staircase leading down. I led the group into the main room of the cellar and, while it was cold outside, the level of chill in the air was something indescribable. It seemed that from the main room there were smaller rooms attached that were being used for storage. I could clearly see the outline of a coffin and I have to admit that it startled me. The manager explained to me that it was used as a Halloween prop for the house and I breathed a sigh of relief. I also explored a small room in the back of the basement that was being used for laundry and food storage and there was something about it that made me feel uncomfortable, so much so that I couldn't stay there for long.

I returned to the main room where the group was standing and set up the ghost box on a small table. This was the second-generation design, and while it was smaller than the first, it was still large and cumbersome. The device was black and had a handle on it, but I still had to use an extension speaker so that we could hear the machine. Everyone stood around the table, as I got ready to turn on the device. I could see that the students were anxious and uncertain about what was about to take place.

I flipped on the power switch and within seconds, voices started to come through the speaker of the machine. The reality of the situation affected the group deeply and I could clearly see that some of them were scared. My mother walked throughout the group reassuring them with a smile. As the voices started to become more clear, I said, "Lizzie, are you there?" In my haste to communicate with Lizzie Borden, I completely forgot the protocol of connecting with a Spirit Technician first, and put myself in great danger.

Several seconds went by while gibberish came through the speakers before a dominant male voice made itself heard. While the voice didn't make much sense at first, it quickly became clear enough to understand. The entity learning to use the machine was extremely strong and independent. Before I could utter another word, the entity began to curse me out in a deep New England accent in a way that I had never experienced. I was stunned by what was coming through the speaker and when I took a step back and looked at the group, they were even more shocked than me. The language was so coarse that several people stepped back and some even left the room. All at once, I realized the entity I was communicating with was, in fact, Andrew Borden. I mistakenly assumed he thought we were there to disrespect him, so I started to speak over the top of him. I said, "Mr. Borden, I'm so sorry. We are not here to disrespect you in any way, we only want to find out what truly happened that day and hopefully bring you peace." He immediately resumed cursing me out in an insane barrage of profanity last heard circa 1900.

I was dumbfounded and didn't know what to say. I called on the Spirit Technician to assist us and, while she did become part of the conversation, she was unable to take full control of what was taking place. Mr. Borden remained a fixture in the background. Fortunately, we were able to communicate with Bridget the maid, as well as Lizzie Borden herself. The reason for Mr. Borden's rant soon became clear as the facts came to light.

According to the spirits speaking through the device, Mr. Borden's miserliness was the least of his crimes. Apparently, he'd been sexually abusing both of his daughters for a good part of their lives. He wasn't feeling disrespected. No. He was concerned the truth was going to come out through Frank's Box! He was still trying to protect his dirty secret! Hearing this, and being a father myself, I became enraged. While I preach being respectful to all spirits, I was completely unable to control my anger and rage. I began to argue with Andrew Borden and eventually it turned into a screaming match. Those that remained from the group stood by in shock as Andrew and I exchanged verbal blows back and forth. As things became heated, my mother calmed me down enough to end the session. There I stood, with my hand still on the power switch of the device, in complete disbelief at what had just taken place.

There was silence in the room for quite some time, as no one knew what to say. We packed up the equipment and went back upstairs to the kitchen where we discussed what happened to the remainder of the group. My mother and I were deeply disturbed at the exchange that taken place, but some of the people who witnessed it seemed charged from the interaction. Everyone who was there that night was able to hear an account of the atrocities that had had taken place in the house from the actual spirits who had lived it. As each person left, either to their rooms or back to their homes, they were left with an experience they would never forget.

My mother and I decided it was time to get some sleep. It was late and the museum opened early the next morning and we would have to be out of our room when it did. We said good night to the manager and her friend and made our way up the stairs to Andrew Borden's bedroom. I was completely drained of energy and just wanted to get a few hours of sleep before we had to leave. As I closed the main door to the stairs, my mother looked at me with exhaustion and unease in her eyes.

I said, "See you in the morning. Oh wait, it's already morning." We both laughed as I made my way to the dressing closet. I flipped on the light and closed the door behind me. I was so tired. I quickly got ready for bed, turned off the light, and got under the covers. As I lay there in Mr. Borden's room in the Lizzie Borden House, my eyes quickly adjusted to the dark. Streetlights illuminated small aspects of the corners of the room. I stared up at the ceiling and felt complete shock and disbelief at the rage and profanity-filled exchange I'd had earlier that evening with Andrew Borden via Frank's Box.

After a while, fatigue took over and I tried to get comfortable in the bed. As I rolled over onto my left side, I clearly heard a man's voice whisper: *Don't turn your back!* Once I started breathing again, I tried to calm down, attempting to convince myself that it was my imagination. I thought about where I was, the site of a double axe-murder homicide—not to mention the disturbing, emotionally charged confrontation I'd had with Mr. Borden downstairs and in whose room I was now attempting to sleep. After a few minutes of lying there, I decided to attempt sleep again, this time on my right side. As I was drifting off, I felt a cold breath on my ear and heard a more emphatic warning: *Don't turn your back!* I slept on my back that night.

At some point during the night I woke to my own desperate gasps for air. Something tightened around my throat, cutting off my air supply—but when I reached out for whatever it was, there was nothing. Panicked, I sat up and started lashing out at the air around me, falling out of bed in my frantic attempt to breathe...

I was losing consciousness when something clicked, and all at once I convinced myself I was having a waking nightmare. Suddenly the pressure released from around my neck and I took in a long, deep breath, gasping and choking for a few more moments. Drained of all my energy, I fell forward into the bed in front of me and slept until the alarm went off. When I opened my eyes, I saw sunlight shining through the window and I thought, "I didn't think I was ever going to see that again!" As I lay there for a few minutes, I attempted to rationalize what happened the night before. Since I was looking for the most logical explanation, I assumed it must have all been a bad dream.

I eventually got up, dressed, and made my way out of the room. As I opened the door, I was startled to see my mother standing right in front of me. Her eyes were dark and it looked like she had gotten less sleep than I had. I asked, "What happened to you?"

She replied, "All night long somebody just kept saying over and over: *Don't turn your back, don't turn your back!*"

Stunned, I exclaimed, "Oh my God! I had the same experience. That's the same thing that happened to me!" As we discussed our shared experience, she suddenly stopped talking and a shocked expression took over her face. I asked, "Are you okay?"

She continued to stare and suddenly raised her arm and pointed toward my head. In an extremely stern voice, she asked, "What happened to your neck?"

"What are you talking about?" I asked.

Louder and almost angry, she again asked, "What the hell happened to your neck?" At this point she began to push me toward the back of the room toward the bathroom. She pushed me in front of the mirror above the sink and I was mortified to see there was a rope burn all the way around my neck. Apparently Andrew Borden decided he was going to end the argument and the use of Frank's Box once and for all.

We don't sleep at the Lizzie Borden House anymore.

CHAPTER · FIVE

The Bereaved Mothers Club

My mom and I were on what we called the "Spirit Phone 2010 Tour" that spanned from Colorado to Minnesota and all the way down through Georgia and Florida when we had one of our most memorable Ghost Box experiences. At that time, we had been on the road for nearly a month and it had been a long drive that had started in Colorado, us stopping and performing at countless metaphysical centers along the way. At each stop we would do a presentation, which would later be known as the Moon Family Psychic Experience. We discussed our hereditary psychic history before doing a public psychic gallery reading, which included tarot cards, psychic counseling, and a demonstration of the Ghost Box where attendees could pose a question to either spirit guides, angels, family members, or anyone else on the other side.

At these events, people signed up for private readings with both my mother and me for the next day. The tour had been extremely successful to that point and we were both very proud of the work and healing we had done. On this particular warm winter day in Florida, we were driving down the highway toward our next tour stop in Fort Myers. Now you have to understand, when I booked this tour I spoke to metaphysical centers and had to determine, sight unseen, if their location would be suitable for our event. Fortunately, most of the stops we made had very nice, clean locations while a few were a bit more questionable.

We never could have imagined what we were going to run into when the GPS directed us to the Fort Myers location. My mother and I looked at each other, completely bewildered, as we drove up to a tall chain-link fence complete with large spools of barbed wire across the top. Behind the fence there was what appeared to be an extremely dingy salvage yard with junk and debris strewn everywhere.

Almost in a daze, I got out of the car and walked up to the fence to find a large padlock protecting all that was inside. I closed my eyes and tilted my head back in pure disgust as if asking the heavens, "Why?" I slowly walked back to the car, got in, and shut the door. I took a moment to collect myself before speaking. "Yeah, the place is locked up."

My mom, always trying to defuse a situation, said, "Well now, let's try not to get upset. Maybe the GPS brought us to the wrong place." Once again we checked the address we had for the center and discovered we were indeed in the right place. I attempted to call the number I used when booking the tour and kept getting voicemail. Even though my mom and I were both upset, we decided to go to the hotel we booked for the night and regroup. We made the decision that we would get ready for the show and hope that a miracle happened. We drove to the location that night and were extremely surprised to find that the gates were open. We drove into the dirt lot and saw there were lights coming from the building off to our left. I parked the car and got out, not knowing what might happen next. As we stepped out of the car, a woman emerged from the building and said, "You must be Chris and Paulette!"

Stunned, we replied, "Um, yes, that's us!" The woman was very friendly and explained to us that the owner's husband had suffered a heart attack and that she was tending to him in the hospital. That was the reason the shop was closed when we arrived earlier. While we both felt terrible about the tragedy that had taken place, we still couldn't quite figure out why the place looked the way it did.

The woman then asked, "Do you have anything you need to bring in?" I explained to her that I just had a small black roller bag in the trunk and other than that, we were ready to go. Interestingly, I noticed there was a fairly large black cat playing with a rooster near the doors to the building. Now this is something you don't see every day and I have to admit my attention was focused on this odd pair. I went to the back of the vehicle, opened the back deck lid, and pulled out my black roller bag. As I extended the handle to start rolling into the building, I was shocked when the black cat jumped on the bag to go for a ride! We all laughed and the woman explained to us that the cat and the rooster were best friends and were kind of like the mascots for this center. I felt like I was in the twilight zone.

When we entered the building, my mother and I were both taken aback at how elegant the retail shop was. The store had a variety of crystals, dream catchers, candles, and other items you find in a high-end metaphysical shop. Though the store was very nice, I didn't see a space where we could perform. I asked the woman where we should set up and she said, "Oh, you're actually going to be upstairs." I didn't even realize there was an upstairs to this location.

We climbed a flight of stairs to the second level and were led into a beautiful, large room that was filled with chairs and sitting pillows. She told us we could set up anywhere we felt comfortable and explained that with the owner's tragedy, she hadn't been able to advertise the event as intensely as she wanted. She said there were only twenty people attending and they were all part of the same club. We completely understood the situation and decided to make the best of it. About twenty minutes later, several older women began to arrive. One by one, they introduced themselves before finding a seat in the chairs we set out. We presented that night and all the women seemed very interested in what we had to say. My mother did her tarot card reading demonstration and several of the women participated, seeming to genuinely gain comfort from the readings. While everything seemed positive that night, we had a distinct feeling of despair within the room so I decided to take a break before doing the Ghost Box demonstration.

While we were on break, one of the women from the group approached me and asked, "Are you aware of what our group is?"

I said, "No, I'm sorry; I'm not." She told me they were a support group for bereaved mothers and that all their children had died in horrific and violent ways. My heart sank as I could only imagine the pain each of them had suffered and then realized how tough this gallery reading might be. I attempted to ground myself to the best of my abilities, gave the group instructions of how the session would work, and then proceeded to turn on the machine. I connected with my Spirit Technician and could sense that he, too, was aware of how unstable the situation might be.

Once I established contact, I reluctantly pointed my finger at the first woman in the group and asked that she state her name. She did and the voice through the machine replied, "Okay, got her." I then asked the woman to give us the name of the person she wanted to reach. She turned her head downward toward her lap and with every ounce of strength and energy she possessed, raised her head and said her deceased daughter's name. There was a few moments of static and radio fragment before a faint young female's voice pushed through the speakers and clearly to all in the room, it said, "Mama?" The mother's head dropped as her tears flowed. The woman next to her gently placed her hand on the sobbing woman's shoulder as if to provide a source of strength and compassion. The woman raised her head to the ceiling and said through tears, "I love you so much." The emotion was felt throughout the space and I don't believe there was a dry eye in the room, including mine.

One by one, I repeated the process for each of the mothers. Each woman had their own unique experience as their children's voices came through the speakers of the Ghost Box. When the last woman communicated with her child and I told the Spirit Technician we were closing down the session, I felt a distinct sense of relief. Never before had I experienced so much raw emotion during one of our gallery readings.

As I sat in the chair with the device on my lap, my mother went to each of the women to provide comfort and reassurance that I believe only one mother can provide to another. I was exhausted and though the room was cooled by air conditioning, I was sweating profusely. I felt I had exhausted all of my energy connecting these lost children with their physical world mothers.

Now in most cases, our hope is that people will have such a great experience during the gallery reading that they want to have a private reading that night or the next day, providing us the money we needed to support the tour. However, on this night we weren't at all interested in conducting private sessions, as all of our energy and emotion had been drained. Hesitantly, I announced that if anyone was interested in a private reading, they could let me know now so we could make arrangements. I was surprised when all of the women in the group said they would like to do private sessions, but they were only available to do it right then and there. They also insisted that the sessions be done in a public setting much like the gallery so they could support one another. My mother gave me a knowing look, as if to say this was something the universe was insisting we do. Without saying a word to each other, we both realized how important this was for these women as well as the spirits of their lost children.

We reassembled the group and the room fell quiet. As I reluctantly flipped the power switch on the device, I called out to my Spirit Technician and he immediately replied. Once again, one by one, we went down the line of women and connected each of them with the spirit of her child. Each communication lasted twenty to thirty minutes. This time the women were able to have full conversations with their kids. Some of the most distinct questions and responses replay in my head to this day. At one point, the third woman in line asked her murdered daughter, "Did you know who he was?" (referring to the despicable killer who took her life). Without hesitation, the girl replied, "Yes! You know him! It was…" The mother's expression hardened and her mouth fell agape. She quickly explained to the room that this was a friend of her daughter and she always felt he was responsible for her death.

In another communication, one of the mothers asked if her daughter had any regrets. The young adult woman replied, "Mom, I'm so sorry. You were right." The mother later explained she'd been concerned about her daughter's drug abuse and knew it would eventually lead to her death. As communication with their children continued, it was apparent this was a support group at a truly deep soul level, and these women were really there for each other.

My mom, initially sitting next to me at the beginning of the sessions, was now standing behind each woman as she received her reading and consoled them while providing energy by laying her hands on their shoulders. It was apparent to me that my mom was being drained as an empath by reliving each tragedy these poor women had suffered. By the time I completed the last session and shut off the machine, I was unsure if I could stand. I reached for a diet soda that sat by my side and drank as much as possible, hoping the caffeine would revive me. It seems it did, as I was able to lift the machine off my lap and set it on a table before slowly standing up. As I got to my feet, I was approached by one of the mothers who grabbed me and hugged me as tightly as she could, thanking me for helping them communicate with their children. I don't remember what I said, but it seemed to be just what she needed to hear. As she released me, another woman was there to embrace me just as tightly, also thanking me for the experience. It didn't take long for me to realize they were not only thanking me, but that they could also sense I still was in touch with their child's energy, allowing them to give their child one last hug. It was one of the most amazing emotional experiences I've ever had in my life.

Once the event wrapped up, the room cleared and my mom and I silently began to pack up our equipment. The employees who initially let us in asked how we thought the event went. The only word I could get out of my mouth was, "Amazing." My mother and I didn't talk much that night on the ride home. I had promised her we would stop by Thomas Edison's Florida home so she could see it, as I'd had an amazing experience there the year before. We did drive by it, but didn't stop—we were simply too exhausted. I started to drive toward the hotel, but instead pulled into the parking lot of a bowling alley within sight of the hotel property. Without saying a word, we walked into the bar area and I ordered us two whiskey and diets. We sat quietly and drank, indulging in several rounds. It wasn't until we drove to the next tour stop the following day that we were able to talk about the incredible experience we'd had the night before. Once again, I realized we had only begun to understand the power of healing that the Ghost Box could provide.

CHAPTER · SIX

ETs, Shadow People, and Other Strangeness

I can't say that I've ever had a particular interest in extraterrestrials but they seem to have an interest in me. My first memorable interaction with extraterrestrials happened when I was in my early twenties. A friend of mine and I were hanging out one night on a street near my house. We were standing by the front of his car talking when I happened to look up in the sky and noticed what I thought was a strange star formation. It looked like an extremely large pyramid or triangle and, though I am no astronomer, I couldn't recall seeing anything like it before. I mentioned it to my friend and he said he saw it as well. We stared up at it for several minutes and then we saw it tilt slowly to the side. Startled, we both said, "Did you see that?" at the same time.

We couldn't believe our eyes as we watched this thing start to move in different directions. I immediately realized that unless someone was staring intently at this object, most people wouldn't have noticed it was there. As we continued to watch, something amazing happened. A small, dim, white circular object emerged from the bottom of the triangle. It descended slowly and then suddenly accelerated toward the ground somewhere off in the distance. My friend and I stood with our jaws agape, watching this unbelievable display. Soon after, another dim light appeared at the bottom of the structure and descended rapidly toward us. Instinctively, we both jumped into my buddy's car as he frantically tried to get the keys in the ignition, fumbling with them for a few moments. That was the last thing I remember.

I started to "come to" sometime later and realized we were several blocks away in front of my neighborhood park. I looked over and saw the keys were still in the ignition, but the car wasn't on. I glanced at the clock on the dash and it was two minutes after the last time I recalled. Confused and fighting a sense of rising panic, I looked at my friend. He sat in the driver's seat, arms at his sides, staring ahead with an odd, blank expression on his face. It took me a few minutes to muster up the words to say his name and ask if he was okay. He didn't respond at first, almost as if we were in different places. I was just getting ready to reach over and push his arm to get his attention when he suddenly looked at me as if I had woken him from a bad dream. It felt like we had been through a grueling ordeal, but we both had absolutely no memory of what happened. We tried to recount our steps from when he was frantically trying to start the car, but neither of us could remember anything from that moment on.

I made my way home in a daze. As I walked through the front door, I noticed it was after 3 am! I had somehow lost not two minutes, but more than *three hours* of time that I can't account for to this day. My mother remembers me being extremely frightened and confused after the events of that night. She said I was traumatized and even feared going out on my own. She said I didn't begin to snap out of it for several weeks. It's interesting—and also ominous—that I have very little memory of that time.

•———•

The Ghost Box has produced incredible results not only from human souls attempting to reach us, but various other non-human spirits. I have had several communications through the Ghost Box with inter-dimensional creatures that most people would call Grey aliens. I never expected to become involved with entities that didn't originate on this planet. This has taught me to keep an open mind going into any and all situations. No one truly knows who the Grey aliens are. They differ from other aliens as we differ from all other species on Earth. When using the device, Grey aliens seem to be the most willing extraterrestrials when it comes to human interaction.

When I had my first Ghost Box interaction with a Grey alien, the sound that came through the device wasn't necessarily English or even words. It was a series of scratchy, popping sounds as well as high-pitched reverberations. I believe the entity was communicating on some sort of telepathic level that most humans have yet to understand. I was only able to interpret the communication because of my mediumship ability—and I was able to determine we were communicating with the *spirit* of an alien entity. It would be one thing to communicate with an alien life form, but to communicate with the spirit of an alien was absolutely incredible. The aliens stated they were no longer living and that they could only communicate with me through the Ghost Box. This exchange reinforced my belief that our universe is truly a spiral, existing in the same space and time but perhaps at different vibrational rates and that all souls, on every level, are somehow connected. The messages I received were not threatening in any way, actually putting me at ease. I think this entity was fascinated with the technology of the Ghost Box and wanted to let us know we were on the right track.

The most memorable encounter I had was when I did an investigation for UFO contactee Stan Romanek. I was called in to do a simple paranormal investigation for Stan, but when my father and I arrived at his residence in Colorado Springs, we were stunned when Stan presented us with a detailed documentary that he was working on. It showed evidence of his abductions and encounters with Grey aliens. After the viewing, my father and I investigated Stan's property and were stunned to find evidence of extreme paranormal activity. Not surprisingly, Stan and Lisa's home had extremely high levels of natural electromagnetic fields or EMF. My father photographed the distinctive face of a Grey alien inside a television that wasn't turned on. I captured hundreds of pictures of spirit orbs throughout the home. We were also able to hear several different voices during open-air EVP sessions. And, we could actually see the images of these creatures in photographs that we took that night.

At the end of the investigation, we turned on the Ghost Box to see if anything came through. We were shocked to hear not only spirit voices, but also what we believed to be alien communication. Once again, we heard the strange sounds that indicated Grey alien communication. Stan picked up several words and I was able to interpret the other sounds. When I relayed messages that were coming through the Ghost Box, Stan confirmed their relevance. Stan was excited to be part of this communication—I believe it brought him relief, even vindication, to know someone else was experiencing alien contact right along with him.

People have asked me how the Ghost Box's Spirit Technician responds to alien energy. The Spirit Technician works as an operator on the other side, and also as a gatekeeper. He or she sometimes—but not always—serves as a translator. They relay to me, the physical medium, who and what we're dealing with. If the Technician feels the communication is a danger to me or to a client, they will shut down the communication immediately. The communication with the Greys stayed open and that was another confirmation they didn't present a threat.

During the Romanek investigation, Stan and Lisa stood nearby and asked questions as well. I don't remember all of the questions they asked, but I do remember Stan asking several questions in an attempt to confirm the bizarre harassment plaguing him at the time and continues to this day. I planned to write an article about what took place, but decided against it due to the strange circumstances and threats that surrounded Stan's case.

During the Ghost Box session, the very clear voice of a British woman came through the machine, telling us to "be careful." Stan explained that this was the voice of the person that would call him on the phone and warn him of impending danger.

At another investigation of Stan and Lisa's home, I was able to validate a shocking experience they'd had: seeing a Grey alien running through their backyard and jumping over fences. We were also able to record a swivel chair in their office moving by itself.

There was one particular incident that happened during a Stan Romanek home investigation that still fascinates me to this day. We were using the fourth-generation Ghost Box in an attempt to communicate with Stan's alien connections. The topic of who or what was behind smearing Stan's reputation came to the forefront. As we started to dig deeply into who exactly was attempting to discredit Stan, an extremely high-pitched sound emanated through the speakers of the device. It was so intense that within minutes we had to turn the volume all the way down and eventually power down the machine. When we turned the device back on, the same ear-splitting screech was back too. We eventually had to give up on that line of questioning. The one question we were able to get through the device during the nails-on-the-chalkboard sound was, "Is there an outside agency attempting to block our communication with you?"

The answer was clear and concise. "Yes."

In my most recent meeting with Stan and Lisa at their home, it was very relaxed and I didn't expect we would be doing a session that night with a few other friends. Luckily, I brought along a new Ghost Box that's so small and portable that I now tend to bring it most places I go. This Box was built by a man named Andre who admired Frank Sumption's work. Andre began to build spirit communication equipment just before Frank passed away in 2014. Andre is a physical medium, which means he has the ability to hear spirits subconsciously. Spirits are able to work through Andre to help build the devices. Frank Sumption was also a physical medium and I believe Andre has picked up right where Frank left off. I've used some of Andre's devices and, though they are different than Frank's Box, I believe they are the next step in Ghost Box technology.

The session I did that night was very casual. I turned on the device and dozens of voices flooded through the speaker. Dina, my then girlfriend and now wife, and I both heard several distinct responses right away and realized our friend Frank Sumption was working as a Spirit Technician (!) at that moment along with two others. This was a very cool moment to have Frank come through the Ghost Box from the other side. Even though Frank and Stan had never met, the alien connection they had was intense. I also found it interesting that I spoke to both Frank and Stan about the other many times, but this is the first time they actually "met."

One of Stan and Lisa's friends was unable to distinguish any of the words coming through the Ghost Box and soon lost interest, leaving the room. The other friend heard almost everything clear as day and was fascinated with the communication. Both Stan and Lisa asked several questions relating to some bizarre phenomenon to which they were being subjected. They were given extremely distinct, specific answers that we believe will help them through the battle that they are facing. They were both grateful for the communication and said they could hear the messages on this device much clearer than on the first two Ghost Boxes they had experienced.

After my initial interaction with Stan Romanek, it seemed I experienced phenomena from another world on a consistent basis. While traveling on my many college tours, I've had interactions with strange lights in the sky and other odd phenomena. I can't begin to count all of the times I've driven along a quiet road in the middle of nowhere in the Midwest and looked up into the night sky to see odd lights and other interesting anomalies. When I called home to tell my wife about the things I experienced, she thought I hadn't gotten enough sleep and was hallucinating.

It wasn't until several years later when we were driving home from a Denver fireworks display on the Fourth of July that I happened to notice a strange mass of lights rapidly moving in bizarre patterns. At first I thought it had to be fireworks or maybe even some sort of skydiving team with flares, but I soon realized that as quickly as these lights fell, they ascended at amazing speeds. I tapped Dina on the shoulder, pointed at the display, and asked her if she could explain it. After watching these lights morph, divide, and then divide again, she had absolutely no explanation and eventually agreed it had to be something not of this world. I felt validated at that moment, but it only deepened the mystery for me.

Many years ago I was conducting one of my Sallie House investigations in Atchison, Kansas. We had spent most of the day investigating the Sallie House, but that night we were invited down to a restaurant just off the river. Once we arrived, we were directed to the basement, which we were told had some sort of ghostly history to it and was the site of bizarre paranormal phenomena.

When we descended the stairs, we saw many strange things that seemed to be out of place. The basement itself was constructed of large stones and, creepily, there were some sort of cages or holding pens along the walls. My immediate psychic instinct sensed something with the Underground Railroad and I turned to one of the employees and asked them if this was indeed the case. They told me that, yes, in fact this had been a location where runaway slaves hid in times of persecution. I took several still photos and could clearly see orb energy throughout the entire basement. We made the decision to go "lights out" and turn on our night vision video cameras to see if we could capture any paranormal activity.

As the lights dimmed, a heavy feeling descended over the room, so much so that it was hard to breathe. I flipped on the infrared switch on the camera and focused on the far back wall, which ran parallel to the river. Only a few seconds went by before we started to see several anomalies come from an invisible point near the wall. At first, it appeared to be standard spirit orbs moving toward the camera at various rates of speed. Soon we started to notice distinct facial structures inside the orbs. In some of the orbs, you could see only the spirit's eyes and then in others, you could actually see the full facial structure coming toward you.

The thing that shocked me and the other investigators was seeing what could only be described as the faces of Grey aliens inside the orb energy. My mother never wanted to talk about aliens and oftentimes women seem to have a deep fear when it comes to the strange creatures, but my mom was actually one of the first people to see the unique faces and point them out. Once we were faced with the new evidence, we conducted an EVP session in the basement location. (This was before we had the Ghost Box.)

I asked several questions as to what we were seeing and why we were seeing it. Guides on the other side informed us that not all energy that we see is what we would consider human energy. We did receive direct communication from the Greys, but it was very jumbled and confusing. It was as if the human entities and alien entities were battling to communicate. It seemed that everyone wanted to talk at the same time and it was a mishmash of sounds and voices.

It was a huge revelation for my mother and I to discover we are part of a much larger community of sentient beings and that when these non-human entities pass away, their spirit energy also uses the same vortex doorways that human energy uses. It was a humbling experience and has definitely changed our outlook on spirit communication and even our place in the universe.

One of the more interesting things we've encountered through the years of investigation is Shadow People. There are many different theories as to what these beings are, ranging from some sort of inter-dimensional time travelers to messengers to demonic entities. I always say if someone tells you he or she is an expert on Shadow People, they're lying. There are no experts when it comes to these creatures.

My mother and I have actually been visited by Shadow People for many years. My mom had her first encounter with a Shadow Person approximately twelve years ago while exercising in her basement. She was on her treadmill watching the TV across the room. As she was walking, she suddenly felt like she wasn't alone. Now, her basement is fairly well known for having paranormal activity, but she said this was something different. She slowly turned her head to the right to look into the darkened bathroom next to her. She said she noticed what appeared to be a dark shadow figure crouching down in the corner of the bathroom. Instinctively she stepped off the treadmill belt and onto the sides of the machine and braced herself. Looking closer at the figure, she noticed it appeared to be wearing clothing of some kind. Frightened, she continued to stare at the figure. She said it was as if the thing suddenly realized she was looking at it and it slowly rose from its crouched position and stood tall. That's when she noticed it looked like it was wearing a long, dark trench coat and a hat resembling a fedora. Once it was fully standing, it raised its arms and ascended directly through the ceiling.

Once the creature was gone, the tension in the room faded and she had a chance to recount everything that had just happened, calling to tell me exactly what had taken place. Never having an experience like that before, it was hard for me to understand exactly what had happened. I went through several different theories in an attempt to classify what this being was, but soon realized it was something we had never dealt with before. (This was at a time when accounts of Shadow People were rare.)

Several years passed, and although we dealt with many different types of entities that we hadn't known existed until we encountered them in our investigations, my mom didn't have any other encounters with Shadow People. That is, up until her father passed away.

One night when she was alone in bed, my mom woke up with a terrible feeling of fear. She thought about her father, who had just passed away, and she felt very sad and alone. She opened her eyes and saw, in the far corner of the bedroom, a dark figure crouched down low. When she sat up to get a closer look, the shadowy figure moved quickly from one corner of the room to another. Then, just as quickly, it moved again to another dark corner, behind and beside her bed.

My mom could then see it was a Shadow Person. She tried to communicate with it, but there was no response. She asked, "What are you doing here? Do you have a message for me?" It then returned to the corner in which she had first seen it.

She then asked, "Do you have a message from my father?" The dark figure telepathically communicated with her that her father had gone on to the other side and all of his suffering was over. My mom felt an overwhelming sense of relief both for her father and herself.

Just like my mom's experience years earlier, the shadow being rose and quickly ascended through the ceiling. Emotion overwhelmed her and she spent the rest of the night crying. Her feelings of fear, sadness, and loss were so intense that she wasn't sure she would live to see the next day. I was completely puzzled by these experiences my mother was having. At this point, I had had no experience with Shadow People myself, but having an inquisitive nature I wanted to experience something, too.

My first experience with Shadow People came while speaking at a conference in Connecticut. Some of the other speakers and I were invited on an after-hours ghost hunt in a popular outdoor park and I decided to take them up on the offer. Dina decided to come along as well. I brought along a camera to see if I could capture any evidence while we were there.

While we were outside examining a wooded area, several of us in the group suddenly felt small rocks hitting us. The pebble projectiles were coming from somewhere within the trees. My first thought was that someone was messing with us, so I ran into the wooded area with a flashlight to see what I could. I looked everywhere but couldn't find signs of anyone nearby. I spoke aloud, asking if there were spirits trying to get our attention. Just as I did, I was struck in the arm by another small rock.

One of the other investigators told me we were probably dealing with Shadow People. (While there are reports of Bigfoot throwing rocks and pebbles, we've also found that Shadow People, being three-dimensional creatures, have the ability to move matter. We still aren't sure if the pebbles being thrown were to communicate with us or to ward us off.) Apparently, this area was well known for this type of activity. As we took more pictures and asked more questions via EVP, we saw shadows effortlessly moving through the trees. The shadows moved at amazing speeds. If we asked a question that struck a nerve with them, they would throw a small rock to get our attention. It was so overwhelming that Dina had to leave the area and go back to the car with a couple of the other investigators because of the intense activity. She was extremely afraid of these entities because of their speed, their ability to move physical matter, and their high level of engagement with us.

The only explanation I came up with for this level of paranormal activity was that there must have been some sort of portal or vortex in that area allowing these beings to come and go at will. I'm still unsure of what their intent was.

My curiosity was piqued by this interaction with Shadow People. I wanted to know more. Over time, while investigating areas that were known to have Shadow People activity, I would turn on the Ghost Box and ask as many questions as I possibly could. The thing I found fascinating was that, when these entities attempted to communicate with us through the device, their responses were high-pitched screeches that were similar to whales and dolphins communicating with one another. I can only listen to it in short spurts, as it quickly becomes painful. Unfortunately, I had no way of discerning what they may or may not have been trying to tell us—my mediumship ability did not help in this instance. I feel confident they are trying to communicate, but again cannot decipher what they are trying to say.

My next experience with a Shadow Person happened at Waverly Hills Sanatorium in Louisville, Kentucky. We were conducting one of our Ghost Hunter University events there during the summer months and had a huge turnout. While we'd investigated this location on our own before and knew there was a huge amount of paranormal activity inside the walls, I couldn't have prepared myself for what happened that night.

While leading one small group through the darkened halls of the building, I was quietly explaining some of the best techniques to capture photographic evidence of an investigation. We didn't have our flashlights on at the time and were simply moving through the halls using the moon as our only light. While there was an occasional flash of the camera, it was nearly impossible to see anything other than shapes as we continued our ghost hunt.

All at once I felt something extremely strange. It's hard to describe, but felt like a deep primal fear overtook everyone in my group, including me. I subconsciously hunched down as if I were preparing for something to happen, but had no idea what it was. As I turned away from my group to look behind us, the smell of dirt and dust filled the air. A huge cloud of debris then rose up from the floor in front of us, causing me to take a step back. As shocking as this was, it was just the precursor to something truly terrifying—a huge black shadow that emerged from the floor and towered over my group and me. I couldn't breathe and I couldn't move. I was frozen. As we all looked up at this massive Shadow Person, it looked back down at us with what I felt was ill intent. In an instant, it turned and ran toward the window ledge off in the distance. All we could do was stand and stare as we watched this imposing entity jump off the ledge to the ground below. We stood shaken for several minutes. Once we gathered our wits, we all ran to the spot the creature jumped from and looked down to the ground. There was no sign of the Shadow Person. To this day we have no idea what these beings are or what their true intent might be.

CHAPTER · SEVEN

JFK and Jackie Kennedy at the Grassy Knoll

Several years ago, we were invited to do a summertime Ghost Hunter University event in Galveston, Texas. I lived in Texas for a short time as a child and I could still remember how incredibly hot and humid it was, so I can't say I was looking forward to making the trip. My mother, father, and I were going, as well as Dina, who was our director of marketing for *Haunted Times Magazine* at the time. We decided that, in order to save money, we would drive rather than fly.

As we started planning the trip, we realized we would travel through the Dallas–Fort Worth area. My mother mentioned that if we had time, we should stop at Dealey Plaza to see if we could pick up anything associated with John F. Kennedy's assassination. We all agreed it would be fascinating to see the site and use the Ghost Box to see if anyone in spirit could give us any specific information about the events of that tragic day. We had no idea what was in store for us—and wouldn't have believed it, anyway, if someone had told us what was going to happen... not until we experienced it for ourselves.

As we made our way out of Colorado and crossed through a small part of Oklahoma before reaching the state of Texas, I realized exactly how long the trip was going to be. The entire state of Texas seemed to be desolate and repetitive. It wasn't a landscape I really wanted to remember, but it is still etched into my brain. It seemed like we drove forever before eventually reaching Dallas that night. We were still doing our *Haunted Times Magazine* radio show at that time and knew we had to reach the hotel to set up the broadcasting gear and get our guest on the air before show time. We set up all of the equipment at the last second and got our guest on the air in time. After a short show, we were able to catch a quick Tex-Mex dinner at a local restaurant. We were all so exhausted that sleep came quickly that night.

The next day we made our way to Dealey Plaza to see if we could contact someone on the other side who had been there on November 22, 1963, and knew what truly happened. We eventually found a parking spot right behind the famous grassy knoll. As we got out of the vehicle and started walking toward the legendary site of the shocking national tragedy and birthplace of so many conspiracy theories, my mother told us about her first visit to this location.

She told us that when she first moved to the Dallas area she had convinced my father to take her to Dealey Plaza because she felt compelled to experience the place where Kennedy was shot. It was important to her to be able to be in that exact spot to attempt to empathically pick up on the emotions of that day. When my mom arrived at the book depository, she was overtaken by overwhelming feelings of fear and pain as well as a horrible sense of dread. She had to leave almost immediately, her heart heavy with grief, fear, and despair.

I could sense that, excited as we all were to go into the book depository, there was also a certain hesitation. We crossed the street to walk into the notorious property. At the time, I had no worries or concerns about the small blue Ghost Box I held in my hands. (We were on the third-generation Ghost Box by this time. We called it the Blue Box and it was my primary device for two-plus years. The speaker was very quiet, but it had less static than the previous models, and spirit's words burst through.)

It wasn't until we attempted to enter the building that security guards stopped us and told me I would not be allowed to bring the device inside. I wasn't asked what it was; I was simply told that it wasn't allowed in the building. I remember finding it extremely strange that they were so adamant about me not bringing this device in and yet they didn't have any questions about it. Angry, I thought my day was over at that very moment. My father must have sensed how I felt, because he walked over to me, grabbed the device, and started to leave the property. I knew that, like me, my dad was really interested in going into the depository. I also knew he had to be pretty upset about sitting this one out. When I asked him, my dad said it was more important that I go inside than him and that he would wait outside with the device. Reluctantly, my mom, Dina, and I entered the building. I think all of us felt the sadness that lingered inside the walls of this famous structure. It was an odd tribute to the former president—and in a strange way, to his alleged assassin. There were several films shown about the events that took place that day. To me, it felt almost like propaganda.

As we made our way through the location, we eventually came upon the room that Lee Harvey Oswald sat in on that fateful day. The guide told the story about the rifle Oswald used to shoot JFK from the large window. We had to look at the room through Plexiglas, as it was being historically preserved. As I looked around the room, I could feel, at a deep level, that something wasn't adding up. I think the three of us knew at that point there was more to the story. As we readied to exit the building, our tour guides showed our group one final film about JFK and the events of that day, almost trying to cement in our collective minds the official story of what had taken place.

The three of us left the building and found my father out on the sidewalk. He asked us what had taken place inside and all of us were at a loss for words. My dad handed me the device and as he did, we decided to walk to the grassy knoll and see if we could reach spirits who might be able to shed light on what truly took place that day. It was an odd feeling, standing at this famous location, Ghost Box in hand, preparing to speak to someone on the other side about such a pivotal historic event.

We stood on the knoll looking down at the spot, clearly marked on the street, where the president had taken his last breath. (We find ourselves in some interesting positions with the paranormal investigative work we do, but this moment may have been stranger than all the others combined.) The four of us huddled together and I flipped the small black switch on the front of the device. "Technicians assist," I said out loud. My eyes scanned the area around us to see if anyone was listening. At this point, no one had any idea or interest in what we were doing. Suddenly, through the white noise that was roaring through the small speaker on the box, my Spirit Technician answered and let me know we were prepared for safe communication.

I can't remember my exact words that day, but they were something along the lines of, "Is there anyone there who can help us understand what truly took place in this location when John F. Kennedy was assassinated?" Some time went by without any answer. Feeling somewhat exposed (because the location was so public), and also a little self-conscious, we were about to give up on the idea that we might communicate that day. Suddenly, an extremely familiar-sounding voice burst through the speaker. Our minds raced trying to decipher who it was. We all scrambled, talking over each other, attempting to put two and two together when it dawned on me that the Boston dialect coming through was that of none other than John F. Kennedy. We looked at each other in amazement and disbelief.

It took me several seconds to compose myself and think about posing a question to this great man. "Um, Mr. President, I mean John, sir!" Because it had never occurred to us that JFK might come through the Ghost Box, I had no idea how to properly address him. Before I could ask my first question, the former president started providing us with definitive information about what had taken place that fateful day. He knew the reason why he had been killed and who the secondary gunmen was. He gave us in-depth details about the conspiracy behind his assassination.

Dina feverishly took notes of everything that was said. She transcribed every detail and even asked the president to repeat certain facts to make sure we heard them correctly. Keep in mind that, while this communication was taking place, we were standing outside in the daytime, in the very spot where JFK had been assassinated. It was at that moment my father looked up and noticed three men standing approximately fifteen to twenty feet away from us, well within hearing distance of our Ghost Box session.

My dad casually tapped me on the shoulder and mumbled under his breath to me to look at the three men. The first thing I noticed was the odd way they were dressed. All three were wearing white long-sleeved dress shirts and multicolored Bermuda shorts as well as black dress shoes with long black socks pulled up to their knees. Each of the men wore a dark pair of aviator sunglasses.

My focus was then pulled back to the session when I heard another extremely recognizable voice come through the speaker of the machine. It was Jacqueline Kennedy Onassis! She immediately told us that she was worried about the children. We were confused by the statement but felt that Jackie must have been referring to her children John and Caroline. She also talked about Bobby Kennedy and his voice actually came through for a short time as well.

Here is the exchange as it was written in Dina's notes. (This is immediately after JFK came through.)

Chris Moon: We want quick answers about his death.
Spirit Technician: Yes, about his death.
CM: Where did the shot come from?

ST: Shot from behind the fence. First was a warning shot to scare JFK.

CM: Who was involved in this plot?

ST: Mob, American Government, KKK. Oswald was told he was to shoot only to scare JFK.

CM: Why did they do this?

ST: Against civil rights. Murder.

Jackie Kennedy: We are at risk! Watched! Know about the voices... only five who know!

ST: Lyndon Johnson was not involved.

JFK: I was worried about Jackie's safety.

JK: I was concerned about the convertible.

JFK: I told her that it (would) be OK.

JK: I knew that John was with me after his death.

JFK: Lee Oswald was a decoy.

ST: Man behind fence shot JFK dead.

JFK: Hoffa not involved.

ST: Man who killed JFK was with the CIA. He was hired by several different agencies. (Mob, CIA, KKK.)

JFK: Secret Service was involved! Just one person helped to plan route to make it easy access for the shot.

JK: Watch out!

ST: John crossed quickly. Faith helped him cross. I saw him. Went right through!

Bobby Kennedy: Ted will not be elected.

JFK: Bobby was assassinated because he reopened the investigation.

JK: These two bastards up top Jack Beauvior?

JK: Daddy! Stop!
JK: *Run!!!*

At some point in the conversation, a certain tension came through the device and the energy shifted all around us, as if the very air took on a totally different feeling. The voices that came through the box sounded hurried and urgent. I could feel the tension radiating through my arms to the point they ached.

We were so fascinated with speaking to the Kennedys that we lost track of the oddly dressed men. It was at that moment I felt my mother lightly kick the front of my shoe. It broke my concentration long enough for me to look up and see the three strange men were basically on top of us. At that very moment, Jackie Kennedy's voice screamed through the speaker: *"Run!"*

I immediately shut down the session and we sprinted back to our vehicle. Once we got into the car, we locked the doors, started the car, and sped away quickly. As I drove, Dina continued to write down as many notes as possible and record all of the things that we heard and experienced that day. We were on the highway moving toward Houston when I looked in the rearview mirror and saw a black suburban with tinted windows behind us. At first I didn't think much of it, but over time, as I switched lanes, it was obvious it was following us.

We drove for quite a while before we looked back and saw the vehicle was turning around and going back the other way. While we were being followed, it felt like we were in some sort of nightmare or bad movie. Adrenalin is the only thing that kept my mind in the moment and allowed us to escape. I don't believe that it was simply a scare tactic; I honestly believe that if the opportunity had presented itself, we would have been abducted.

CHAPTER · EIGHT

A Gangster, a President, and Other Ghouls in Illinois

Over the years, I have had hundreds of encounters with famous people who have passed. Two of the most memorable experiences took place in Illinois.

The first was an exchange with President Lincoln while in Springfield. I was scheduled to do a public Ghost Box gallery reading at the Ile's House and Museum of Springfield History, which once belonged to Lincoln's parents' friends. When I arrived at the location, a woman who was the curator of the museum greeted me. She was very skeptical and asked me several times if I could really communicate with the other side. I assured her I could and encouraged her to take part in the gallery reading. The event was held in the basement of the house. I sat at the front of the room with the device on a table while a few event organizers sat with me. The room was set up in a semi-circle, attendees facing me.

When I turned on the machine and established contact with my Spirit Technician, I began to let the audience ask their questions. At most events, people want to communicate with their loved ones who have passed but this time around, the majority of people wanted to reach President Lincoln. I attempted to make contact with him but first, we were greeted by Lincoln's wife, Mary Todd Lincoln. She was loud and boisterous and bragged about the museum that had been erected in the President's honor. That is when we heard the humble voice of Abraham Lincoln come through for the first time. He didn't sound like anyone expected him to, his voice more tenor than anything else, but it carried with it a huge presence that commanded respect. Quickly, stunned attendees started to ask him questions and it turned into a makeshift presidential press conference. "Mr. President" led every question and he graciously answered everyone. One of the audience members asked, "Mr. President, Mr. President, how do you feel about Obama becoming president?" There was a short pause before Lincoln replied, "It is my proudest moment. That is my legacy." The room erupted with intrigue after his response.

When we reviewed the night vision videotape of the event later, we could clearly see a spirit orb fly in and circle over my head during his response, which was great validation. After our exchange about President Obama, the curator spoke up from the back of the room and asked, "How do we know that this is really President Lincoln?" There was silence over the device for a few seconds before I heard the President's voice respond, "Coat rack."

I was puzzled by the response but the curator pushed me for the answer. Sheepishly, I responded, "Coat rack. He said coat rack." The woman's face went white as she turned her back and left the room. After I finished the reading, I stood in the basement chatting with some of the attendees when I noticed the curator walking toward me. She was holding something in her hands. She walked quickly and I realized she carried a good-sized piece of wood. Panicked, I thought she was going to hit me with it. She walked up to me and motioned for me to hold out my hands. Instinctively, I did. She set the object in my hands. I was baffled. She asked, "Do you know what that is?"

I responded, "No."

In a shaky, but matter-of-fact tone, she said, "That is the coat rack that Abraham Lincoln hand carved for his parents. We keep it hidden away in one of the closets upstairs. No one knows it's here." This experience confirmed for me the importance of repeating exactly what the spirits say, no matter how outlandish it may sound to me.

Another encounter with an infamous Illinois resident occurred many years ago when some of our staff members from *Haunted Times Magazine* invited us to Illinois to scout out possible Ghost Hunter University locations. We flew into Chicago's Midway Airport and based ourselves at a nearby hotel. At the time we had no idea the first location our staff wanted us to see was well over two hours away! We drove out of the city and were soon treated to acres of barren land and highway.

Our first stop was a location known as Ashmore Estates. We met our staff members along the way and took two cars to the location. We followed them through several small towns, wondering if we were ever going to reach our destination. Eventually, we came upon what looked like an old, abandoned building with a modern doublewide trailer nearby. After getting out of the car, we were met by the property owner who immediately began to attempt to tell us the entire history of the building. We had to stop him mid-sentence, quickly explaining that if he gave us too much information on the history and paranormal activity, it would taint any investigation we would conduct. I think he was a little taken aback by us cutting him off, but he soon seemed to relax.

Walking into the building, I can't say I immediately felt much activity. We took several pictures and used our EMF detector to see if we could pick up any electro-magnetic spikes inside the building. Soon, we saw positive signs of spirit activity when orbs appeared in our pictures. The thing we found most interesting is that we actually heard voices inside the building—and they were very clear. I have to admit that at one point I started to wonder if someone was hiding in the building, attempting to make us think it was more active than it really was.

I eventually pulled out the Ghost Box and did a session where I communicated with the spirit of a younger woman who told me she had been a patient inside the facility. As I relayed information coming through the device, the owner nodded his head in agreement. I could tell by his demeanor that the voices coming through the machine made him extremely uncomfortable. I believe he had been confident his property was haunted, but the reality of hearing the spirit voices was something he wasn't prepared for.

After conducting an open-air EVP session and taking several more pictures, we decided to go outside and discuss business. It really is funny looking back on it, but the owner seemed like he was dazed. While we were talking projections and figures, he seemed to be trapped in the moment when he heard the first voice come through the Ghost Box. After looking at some initial dates to do an event, we parted ways.

The next day, our employees took us to several purportedly haunted locations throughout the Chicago area. My expectations were high, having heard all the amazing stories that had taken place in and around the city, but by the end of the day I felt extremely disappointed with the lack of activity we experienced. It wasn't until that night we encountered some actual spirits. Sometime around 7 pm, our staff took us out to the road where people saw the famous spirit of "Resurrection Mary." This legend is said to have sprung from the true story of a young woman named Mary who was at a local dance hall with her boyfriend in the late 1930s. They got in a fight at the dance and Mary left the hall, intending to hitchhike home. Unfortunately, she never made it—she was struck by a car and killed. Mary's parents and boyfriend were heartbroken. She was buried at Resurrection Cemetery, just a few miles from where she died. Mary's spirit is said to wander along the road in an endless attempt to get home. There have been many reported sightings of Resurrection Mary over the years; she is described as a beautiful young blond woman who appears and disappears into thin air.

The Resurrection Mary road was absolutely teeming with activity. Almost every picture came back with positive evidence of spirit in the form of mists and orbs and my psychic Spidey senses were off the chart! I could've stayed there for hours, but the others were anxious to take us to a location nearby they believed we would really enjoy.

We soon arrived at an older, average-looking building that seemed to house some sort of restaurant or bar. As we walked in, my mother and I looked at each other. Both of us were experiencing the same sort of psychic impression. "There have been a lot of deaths here," she whispered.

I replied, "You're getting that too?" Before we could see any more, two men approached us and introduced themselves as the owners of the property. They were friendly but didn't give us much information about the property and I appreciated that. They looked at each other knowingly and then told us to feel free to take a look around.

All the team members carried small pieces of equipment, but my father focused on using his camera to see if he could capture any evidence. He snapped a picture and immediately looked at the viewfinder to see if there was anything there. Very early on, he showed us different bits of evidence, from orbs to anomalous mists and even some strange shadows. As we walked through the location, it was an eclectic, almost jarring mix of the old building and its energy along with several different modern elements, such as neon signs advertising beer and other products. To be honest, it was a little bit confusing to me. I felt like spirits were reaching out to speak to me, but they seemed extremely confused and almost afraid to say anything.

My mom stayed close by my side as we ventured throughout the building. After twenty minutes or so, we met back up with the owners and asked if there were any other locations we could investigate inside the building. They said, "Yeah. Want to come upstairs and see what you can find?" As we ventured up the staircase, I started to feel that familiar sensation of energy being drained from my body. It started on my shoulder as a pinching sensation and was soon followed by a numbness and fatigue throughout my body. Soon my head began to feel very light and my chest tightened. I turned to my mother to say something, but before I could open my mouth she could see my eyes drooping and knew exactly what was happening. She grabbed my arm, attempting to give me some of her energy so I could continue to ascend the stairs. I don't remember climbing the last set of steps, but I do clearly remember walking into a dark room at the top. My father continued to snap pictures, excitedly commenting about how many orbs he was capturing. I definitely felt this room was the source of the activity in the building.

We decided it was time to fire up the Ghost Box to see if any of the spirits wanted to communicate. As I turned on the device and started communicating with my Spirit Technician, I could already hear several lost souls attempting to communicate through the machine. The Spirit Technician assisted by telling us that this property was originally a speakeasy in the 1920s. When I relayed this information, the building's two owners got wide-eyed. I asked the question, "Who used to run this place?" There was a moment of static and silence and then one word came through the speaker of the device: *Caponi*. I turned to the team and the extremely confused owners, and said, "Did you guys hear that? It said Caponi."

Before I could say anymore, the same voice came through the machine and nearly yelled "Frank Caponi!" The owners looked so stunned I thought they might pass out.

I quickly asked, "Does this make any sense to you at all?"

One of the men looked directly in my eyes and said, "Frank Caponi. Do you know who that is?"

I said, "No."

He continued, "Everybody's heard of the Capones, the famous gangsters."

I replied, "Yeah, of course."

He said, "Their name was actually Caponi. They changed their name when they came to the United States." I was still a bit puzzled. He went on. "Frank Capone—he's the one that used to own this place."

I was frozen with fear. Not only did we have this amazing communication and confirmation, but we were directly in contact with the spirit of one of the most famous gangsters in American history. It was so unsettling to me I had to shut down the device to collect myself. I reconfirmed all the information with the owners just to make sure I truly understood what was taking place. They reiterated all the facts that came through the device and said they were blown away. "This is like one of those TV shows!" one of the owners exclaimed.

I reiterated, "We get some great communication and confirmation through this machine but even I am stunned by this one!" After a few minutes we decided to turn the Ghost Box back on to see if we could gather any more information. We were soon in contact with several spirits that had been murdered inside the building.

Apparently the room we were standing in had once been Capone's office. If there was a problem with someone in the family or organization, the person was brought to that room and many times disciplined or even snuffed out right then and there. Some of the spirits made reference to their bodies still being in or around that location. We spoke to Frank several times during that session, and unlike many spirits we speak to, his voice and personality were just as you imagined it to be. He was unapologetic for his crimes and looking back on it, I don't feel he saw them as crimes at all. I believe he just thought of it as "doing business."

We ended the session with more questions than answers, but all of us in the room that night felt as if we had somehow ventured into the past and spoken to a living legend. The owners thanked us repeatedly for coming in and doing the investigation and offered us the location for one of our Ghost Hunter University events.

They were in the middle of a renovation in the building and I believe the commotion and upheaval sparked the paranormal activity. Soon after we visited, we attempted to contact them by phone. Unfortunately, they sold the business to someone else and the new owners weren't interested in ghosts, not even the ghosts that still haunt the property to this very day. I hope that one day we can return to that building and help some of the lost souls that feel like they're trapped there—and maybe even have one more chance to speak to the notorious mafia boss Frank Capone.

CHAPTER · NINE

Unsolved Murders at the Lumber Baron Inn

I was sitting at the desk in my office at the newly formed *Haunted Times Magazine* when I received a phone call. There was a woman on the other end of the line, desperately trying to tell me about an encounter she and her husband had just experienced at a bed and breakfast in Denver. I interrupted her and asked, "Wait, did you have a paranormal experience there?"

She almost yelled, "Yes!"

I thanked her for calling and told her that we would check it out. I looked up the phone number of the business online and made a quick call.

"Hello, Lumber Baron Inn," said the male voice on the other end of the line. I explained who I was and asked for the owner. The man said that he was, in fact, the owner and I told him about the call I received a few minutes earlier. He began to tell me about the ghost of the Lumber Baron Inn and I immediately interrupted him. He seemed a bit annoyed, but I quickly explained to him that if we were to do an investigation, it would skew my views of the property to know anything ahead of time. He said he understood and agreed to let us come out a few nights later to investigate.

The team of investigators was small—just me, my mother, and my father—but we felt we could get the job done. Pulling up to this property in the old Highlands neighborhood in Denver, the immense and impressive Victorian mansion stood out like a diamond in comparison to the other houses. As we got out of our Jeep and started to unload equipment, my mom and I both began to sense at least one presence in or around the house. For me, the energy there was a bit more confusing than anything I'd experienced. I usually start to get some sort of impression about what may be attempting to communicate, but in this instance it was all very hazy. Both my mom and I discussed feeling some sort of oppression or depression surrounding the property, but neither of us could put our finger on what it was. A large metal fence surrounded the house and the gate made a screeching sound as it slowly swung open—like something out of a horror movie. With the cold night air and darkness as our backdrop, you couldn't help but feel a bit creeped out about walking into this place.

We climbed the steps to the front porch and pushed the call button on the intercom at the front door. Only a few moments passed before we heard the inner door slowly creak open and then the large outer wooden door opened. There stood the man I talked to on the phone and he cordially invited us in. Walking into the house was like going back in time. There was a large, ornate wooden staircase in front of us, while off to the left you saw what appeared to be some sort of parlor. Also in front of us was what appeared to be either a dining room or library, maybe both. The enormity of this mansion was immediately evident. The man told us he had done quite a bit of work to restore the house back to its original condition and it was obvious he had spent a lot of money. He seemed to be a very nice gentleman with a very theatrical flair.

I decided the best course of action for the investigation was to have my mom spend time talking to the owner while my father and I did the bulk of the initial investigation. We went lights out in the house and decided it was best to only bring handheld devices that were easy to carry. We brought cameras, EMF meters, a crude night vision video camera, as well as digital and tape voice recorders. While we had the original Ghost Box in our possession at the time, we still didn't believe it worked so it was sitting on a shelf back at the office.

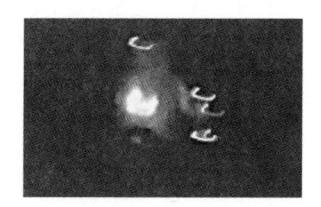

Photographic evidence of the green demon at the Lumber Baron Inn.

We decided we would start our investigation at the top of the house, in the third floor ballroom. My dad walked through the room with the 3.2-megapixel digital camera over his head randomly snapping pictures. I think he was surprised by the amount of spirit orb activity he was capturing. I decided I would attempt to do an open-air EVP session to see if I could get any responses. I started the session by turning on the recorder and speaking to any spirits that may have been in the room with us. Just as I was saying, "I'm speaking to the spirits that we cannot see..." I was interrupted by an older gentleman grumbling somewhere in the room. Initially, I thought it was my father saying something, so I shined my flashlight directly at him. He looked back at me and shook his head as if to say it wasn't him. Even though my father was skeptical, he was respectful of the investigation process and I knew he wouldn't lie to me about this. I also saw a bit of unease on his face and felt he may have heard what I had. As I continued the session, I asked questions and there were several disembodied voices in the room I couldn't logically explain. Each time I shined my flashlight back toward my father, I could see he was becoming more and more uncomfortable. As I ended the EVP session, we heard a large bang in the turret room just off the ballroom. Both of us jogged to the area, but once again could find no logical explanation for the sound we heard.

We investigated the first floor for quite some time and, other than a few spirit orbs caught on camera, there wasn't much activity. We returned to the second floor and investigated all of the guestrooms. We went room by room, taking pictures and occasionally stopping to do an EVP session, but weren't getting many results that we could see or hear at that time. We started to walk back toward the staircase and noticed a room that had a placard on it that said, "Valentine Suite." For some reason, I was immediately drawn to this room.

As we walked in I shined my flashlight around the room and could see all the walls were red and there was an ornate chimney on the far wall. The large bed in the center of the room took up quite a bit of space. There was a new bathroom on the left-hand side of the room as well as a nice Jacuzzi tub under the window. There were also a few random pieces of furniture that filled the remaining space. The room had a distinct energy and to me felt extremely cold. There were streetlights shining in from the window and the flash of my father's camera bounced off the window and the mirror just in front of me. I felt sad for no apparent reason and it was almost as if the room itself needed to talk.

In a quiet voice, I told my father to please pick a spot to stand still. I felt like I needed to do an EVP session. My dad stood near the tub and window in front of me and I felt compelled to sit on the bed. I pulled out my digital voice recorder and fumbled for the "on" switch. Once I was able to push the button, the recorder responded with a light on the display. I centered the recorder in my palm and with my other hand prepared to push the record button when I heard a female voice scream in my ear, "Get out! Get out! Get out!" I jumped from the bed, dropping the recorder somewhere on the floor. It startled my father and he took several steps toward me asking what happened. I fell to my knees searching for the recorder I dropped. Reluctantly, I reached underneath the bed, my arm flailing wildly in an attempt to find the lost device. My fingers finally touched something and I realized it was the recorder. I grabbed it and got to my feet as fast as I could. I picked up the camera I'd set on the bed and stuck it in the pocket of my vest. Without saying a word, I raced down the large staircase and out the front door. My father was right behind me and once we made it out front, he began to question me on what happened. I was extremely shaken and told him about the voice I heard. Even though he was an extremely skeptical man, I think he saw the shock and fear in my eyes and knew I was telling the truth. It took me a few minutes to compose myself before we were able to meet up with my mother and the owner. My mom conducted an interview with him while we were doing our investigation. My father set up his laptop and downloaded pictures and audio. My mother was a mediator in our disclosure of what we had discovered during the investigation of the Lumber Baron Inn.

We told the owner about our experience on the third floor and the loud banging sound we heard in the turret room. My mother smiled and laughed a little bit as she said to him, "Can you please tell them about what you told me happens up there?" The owner went on to tell us that his son, who was about seven years old at the time, stayed with him half the time and with his mother the other half. His son seemed to enjoy the house and explored it quite often. Apparently he used to get upset with his son for leaving fingerprints on the rounded windows of the third-floor turret room after being warned not to touch the glass several times. The boy swore he didn't touch the glass, but it was obvious he was the only culprit.

One day the owner went to go clean upstairs and once again found the fingerprints on the windows. It was then he realized his son couldn't have been the one to leave the fingerprints, as he hadn't been there for a couple of weeks. My father turned the laptop toward the owner and showed him an outdoor picture of a bright spirit orb next to the turret as well as what appeared to be a full-bodied apparition in the window. When we took that picture, there was no one upstairs. The owner seemed a bit disturbed but also intrigued by our findings. As we continued to download evidence, I told him about the experience I had in the Valentine Suite. I was still shook by it and that intensity came through in my description. As I relived the event, I looked at my mother and her wide eyes seemed shocked by what I was saying. As I glanced toward the owner, his eyes narrowed and he had a look of disbelief on his face. I quickly told him, "This really happened! My father is a witness!"

The owner looked at me and basically accused me of doing research on the house, which of course I hadn't. I asked, "Does this make any sense to you?"

He looked at me in a very odd way and said something like, "Obviously it does." Then he told us what had taken place in the location now known as the Valentine Suite many years earlier. The October 13, 1970, headline of the *Denver Post* newspaper read "Teen Girls Found Slain in Denver Apartment." Seventeen-year-old Cara Lee Knoche and eighteen-year-old Marianne Weaver were found murdered in what is now the Valentine Suite of the Lumber Baron Inn. Cara Lee was sexually assaulted and strangled, her nude body crammed underneath the bed. Apparently her friend Marianne, the mother of a small child, walked in on the crime taking place and was found lying on the bed with her arms folded across her chest and a single bullet hole in her head. At that time, the Lumber Baron Inn had been run down and was being used as low-rent apartments. Though the police quickly tried to make the girls look like hoodlums, stating they had found marijuana and a pipe in the apartment, the girls both came from affluent families. According to Cara

Lee's father, a doctor had recommended the use of marijuana for her seizures. The police painted Cara Lee as a runaway, but she had her parents' consent to live there and had planned to move back home just days after the horrific crime happened.

The person who discovered the crime scene was a friend of both girls. Apparently he had been driving by the building in the early morning hours and noticed the light was off in Cara Lee's apartment window. According to the young man, he went into the building, climbed the stairs, and found the door to the apartment ajar. As he pushed it open, he said all the lights were off inside the room, but he could see the silhouette of someone lying on the bed. This is when he discovered Marianne's body on top of the bed and saw Cara Lee's foot sticking out from underneath the bed. Apparently there wasn't a pay phone inside the building, so the young man had to run down the street to find a pay phone and contact the police. The crime scene was botched and appears to have not been taken seriously. A killer was never identified and the case remained unsolved.

As the owner relayed the story to me, many of the events that took place in the Valentine Suite that night started to make sense. When I heard the spirit screaming, "Get out!" in my ear, I had assumed it was a spirit telling me to leave that location. I quickly realized it was a spirit recounting what had taken place on that terrible night, maybe doing so knowing I might be able to understand. We asked the owner if it was all right if we came back to investigate with the goal of helping the girls. He agreed and we said good night.

On the drive back to South Denver, my mother and I discussed how amazing it was that these girls were reaching out to us and how incredible it would be if we could help these poor lost souls.

It wasn't long before we contacted the owner and asked to come back to do another investigation. This time around, we focused all of our energy on the Valentine Suite. In our open-air EVP sessions, we explained to the girls who we were and why we were there. We reviewed our evidence in the room on our laptop computers and listened to the voices of the girls as they relived this terrible crime. Within a few sessions, Cara Lee started to respond to some of the questions we asked—it was incredible! After returning from the Sallie House investigation where we used the Ghost Box for the very first time (our fourth investigation of the Sallie House), we decided to attempt communication inside the Lumber Baron Inn.

Once again we focused our investigation on the Valentine Suite and attempted to contact both girls. Everyone on my team was elated when we heard the voice of Cara Lee come through the Ghost Box and we began to use the device to answer very specific questions about the crime. Unfortunately, Marianne seemed to be in a very dark, earth-bound state at this time. Cara Lee answered questions to the best of her ability regarding names, license plate numbers, weapons, and telephone numbers. We were able to document the majority of information that came through the device even though the communication through the Ghost Box was still static-ridden and not very clear. A month or so later, we spoke to the owner of the Lumber Baron Inn about conducting one of our Ghost Hunter University events at the location in hopes someone from the public might be able to come in and ask the right questions. The owner agreed and we set up our first event. It started out small, only 30 people or so, but the attendees who came in seemed determined to help us solve the crime and it quickly gained momentum. Soon afterward, several different local news stations contacted us, asking if they could film our investigations and events in hopes we might be able to find out who killed the two girls. Once the media attention started, the events became much larger. The next event we held had to take place in the ballroom because well over 100 people attended.

I used to start the Ghost Hunter University events by going around the room and having everyone give their first name and state whether they were a believer, a skeptic, or a drag-along. Even though we had a huge number of people, we decided to stick with this practice. When we finally got back to the front row of people, I turned my attention to the next person in line, a pretty blond woman. She said she was a believer and said she actually had a ghost in her own home. She also intended to help Cara Lee and Marianne and hopefully solve the crime. Next to her was her husband, who as I recall was wearing a suit. He told me that he was a drag-along and didn't believe in any of this. Sometime later, I found out the man worked for a Colorado law enforcement agency. I conducted the class that day and, while everyone seemed to have a good time, he didn't really seem interested. He also wasn't impressed with the haunted history dinner.

The group was too large to take everyone into the Valentine Suite at one time to do a Ghost Box session, so we broke the group into several smaller groups. We had wonderful communication with both young women through the Ghost Box and it felt they were making progress in giving us information. When the law enforcement officer's group came in for a session, I was nervous. It turns out he looked into the closed files of the case and was listening for any unknown specific information that might change his stance. As one of the girls spoke through the Ghost Box, each person in the room had a chance to ask a question, including the officer. He had a very specific question and the response that was relayed back surprised him. Apparently it was a fact he was looking for. We spoke to him after the event and he asked if we were interested in unofficially working with him to solve this case. We jumped at the opportunity!

That night he and I did a full-blown interview using the Ghost Box. He asked several questions relating directly to the crime and the girls responded to the best of their ability. As time went by, the officer and his wonderful wife invited me to their home to do Ghost Box sessions and discuss any advancements either one of us had made in the case. He also asked I keep him informed of anything relevant taking place while doing our investigations and events.

At this point, my magazine business had become overwhelming and, in addition to day-to-day literary work, we were also doing Ghost Hunter University events all around the country. Quite a bit of time went by before I was finally able to contact the owner of the Lumber Baron Inn again to ask if he'd be interested in having us do another event. He agreed and we made the arrangements. The classes we held were unique and fun, but several newly formed ghost-hunting groups decided to put on their own events, so it became more difficult to draw attendees.

I decided to place an ad in one of the local Denver papers in hopes it might garner some attention. I was extremely excited about this particular event because I had talked Frank Sumption into doing a live demonstration and history of his Ghost Boxes during the event. Frank was shy and it was difficult to convince him to come out of his workshop, so this was a big deal.

I was manning the phones at the office when I received one of the strangest phone calls I've ever gotten. It was a man who said he saw the ad for the event in the newspaper and wanted to sign up. In most cases when people ask questions about the event, they want to know things like: What's for dinner? How long is the event? Should I bring my own equipment? This man simply said, "Sign me up for your ghost thing."

I was bothered by the man's energy and voice and quickly made a note to myself about this phone call. When the afternoon of the event arrived, I was excited to get back to the Lumber Baron Inn. We had a very nice size crowd and we were once again in the ballroom area. I started the presentation and noticed that everyone was watching except for one man who was sitting alone against the back wall. Once I introduced Frank, I took a step back to listen. Frank was extremely entertaining and talked about how he became involved in building the Ghost Box devices and how we were now working together. He brought a few versions of the machines to give the audience a demonstration of how they sounded differently from one another.

As I stood listening, I could clearly hear one of the girl's voices calling out a man's name through the machine. Realizing the name coming through the speakers was the name of the man sitting by himself, I quietly walked toward him and said,

"Sorry to bother you, but I hear your name coming through the Ghost Box."

The awkward man immediately became flustered and stated, "I have no idea what you're talking about!"

I said, "I know it sounds strange, but I can clearly hear your name coming through the machine."

He then vehemently reiterated, "I don't hear anything! I don't see how you understand any of the noise coming out of that thing!" I could sense his volatility and decided it was best to return to the front of the room.

Once again I stood behind Frank and listened as the girls' voices, as well as several others, pushed through the speakers of the Ghost Box. This man's name emerged several times. Something urged me to the back of the room and confront him again. I gently kneeled down next to him and said in a very low tone, "I'm sorry, but your name is clearly coming through." The man shifted in his chair. It was clear he was uneasy with the situation. All at once, I felt extremely uncomfortable.

He volunteered, "I've never been in this house before!"

Before I could open my mouth, as if something prodded him, he said, "Yeah, so, my mom died recently and I inherited the house just down the street that I grew up in."

All I could say was, "Okay—" before he continued "All right, yeah, so I use to date a girl that lived inside this house … So what?" He quickly folded his arms, looked at the floor, and decided those would be the last words he was going to say.

*This dark demon was captured
via a cell phone camera at the Lumber Baron Inn.*

Once again, I returned to the front of the room to watch the end of Frank's demonstration. I was able to finish my lecture even though my mind was only on the strange behavior of this individual. We got through dinner and eventually were able to take three separate groups into the Valentine Suite to use the Ghost Box to hopefully communicate with the spirit girls. The strange man was in the last group that came into the room. Most people wanted to be as close to the machine as possible to hear things as they came through. This man was quite different, though. He stood as close to the door as possible. I think he was trying to be closest to the door, but unfortunately for him, a few people crowded in behind him. As I always do, I explained to the group I was going to start the session by turning on the machine and attempting to contact my Spirit Technicians for safe communication. I said then, and only then, could we attempt to reach the spirits in the room. Customarily, I rubbed my fingers together in an attempt to ground my energy and then reached for the power switch on the Ghost Box. As I flipped the switch of the somewhat smaller, black generation-two Ghost Box, I could feel the unease within the machine. Hesitantly, I turned up the volume on the front of the device. Just as the sounds from the speakers became audible, the volume shot up beyond my control and before I could say a word, both of the girl's voices started screaming frantically from the Ghost Box, "He's here! He's here!"

The group was stunned by the accusations coming through the machine and I noticed the man in question pushing through the crowd to get to the door. He opened the door and ducked out as the door slammed loudly behind him. As if something had control of my hand, I reached down and shut off the power. Everyone in the room stood in surreal silence, realizing who this man might be.

As time went on, I became more wrapped up with events outside the state of Colorado and the owner of the Lumber Baron Inn began to conduct more murder mystery events at the property. I had all but lost contact with the officer I'd been working with on the case. Looking back on it now, things were appearing hopeless for the poor spirit girls at the Lumber Baron Inn.

In 2010, in one of my rare times at home in Colorado, I received a random phone call at the *Haunted Times Magazine* offices. It was a woman claiming to be an old friend of Cara Lee. She said she heard about the work we were doing to attempt to solve the murders and had also heard how people were speaking directly to the two girls through the Ghost Box. She asked me if it would be possible to do a private reading in the Valentine Suite at the Lumber Baron Inn. I was extremely busy at the time, but knew how important it would be to attempt to put this woman in direct contact with her old friend and how it might positively affect Cara Lee. I contacted the owner and after a few attempts, he found a weeknight when the room wasn't booked, allowing us to come and conduct a session. I can't say I remember all of the particulars that night, but I do recall clear communication between this woman and Cara Lee. It was extremely interesting to listen to them communicate, many times not even needing my interpretation. The woman talked about old times and things they used to do and there were many laughs and tears. I could sense a positive change in Cara Lee's energy and demeanor and realized it would be much easier to speak to her from that point forward. After the session, the woman repeatedly thanked me and said she might be interested in doing another session sometime in the future. Yet somehow I knew she had gotten everything she needed out of that session. There was a definite reconnection and healing that night and it's one of the most rewarding private readings I've ever done.

We only did a few more Ghost Hunter University events at the Lumber Baron Inn with the original owner, as his events became more popular and the spirit girls somehow became an unfortunate afterthought. A development happened several years ago and, if it hadn't been for my mother, I might not have ever known it took place. It turns out the Denver Police Department decided to open up the Lumber Baron Inn murder investigation and turn it into an active cold case file. We wondered if the facts we obtained and provided through the Ghost Box sessions were a contributing factor to this development. We were not in it for the fame or glory, so it meant a lot to us that the police were again focusing on such an important case. We obviously hoped it could be solved quickly.

Fast-forward to late March 2016, my team and I were given an extraordinary opportunity to hold the very first paranormal event at the Molly Brown House Museum in Denver, Colorado. It was a fundraising event attempting to restore the original porch on the house. We conducted our own investigation prior to the event and got some great results. Once the fundraiser was announced, it quickly sold out. The museum was kind enough to give us two dates when we could hold our Ghost Hunter University events at the house in exchange for services during the fundraiser. When I announced the Molly Brown House Ghost Hunter University on social media, it sold out in less than one day. We had hundreds of people who weren't able to get tickets demand a second night. When we checked with the museum, they said unfortunately they weren't equipped for another event that weekend. Soon people asked if I could hold another Ghost Hunter University event somewhere else in the Denver area. I wracked my brain to come up with another great location for an event, but ran into several roadblocks. As people made suggestions of places they would like to investigate, the Lumber Baron Inn came up several times.

I was extremely reluctant to contact the owner, as I knew his focus went in a completely different direction and wasn't sure I could provide a quality event for new attendees. Eventually, I decided it was best to at least give it a try. I called and asked for the owner, but the man on the other end of the phone said he wasn't there. I asked the man if he knew when he would be back and he informed me the former owner had sold the Inn to him and had moved to California. I asked, "Who am I speaking to?"

He said, "My name is Joel Bryant." He went on to explain that he had just taken over. I just happened to glance down at the date on my computer and saw that it was April 1: April Fools' Day! I suddenly remembered attending the former owner's wedding on April Fools' Day in the ballroom many years before. I think I actually laughed out loud on the phone. I thought this was a cool synchronicity and a good sign. I was definitely excited at the new possibilities and I quickly explained who I was and what I wanted to do. Joel listened to me and asked if he could think about it and give me a call back. After giving it some thought for a few days, he agreed. We arranged a meeting down at the Lumber Baron Inn that day to discuss details of the event.

When I arrived at the old familiar building, it felt different somehow; better. I rang the intercom and was met by a friendly man who invited me in. He introduced himself as Joel and we sat down in the old parlor to discuss business. We talked for a few minutes before the energy in the room lightened even more and in walked his lovely wife Elaine holding their grandson. She carried quite a bit of good energy and I could feel the house had somehow adopted that. What started out as a business meeting soon turned toward all things ghosts and paranormal. While Elaine was very open to the spiritual side of things and very much a believer, Joel was more skeptical. Interestingly, though, Joel is extremely empathic and it seemed he had picked up on many of the energies in the house long before I stepped through the door. In our conversation, Joel and Elaine explained that one of their main missions in the house was to make sure the two spirits girls were respected and loved. Not only that, Elaine was determined to solve the murders. I felt like I made an amazing connection with them right away.

They were kind enough to take me up to the Valentine Suite and let me communicate with the girls right away. Though I didn't have any equipment with me that day, I spoke to the girls and something very interesting happened. As I attempted to communicate with them, both Joel and I heard whispering right behind us. I got the impression the girls were thrilled with the new owners and I think they were happy to see me again. We set up all the details for the event and I asked Joel and Elaine if we could return with equipment and try to speak with the girls again. They both agreed.

I returned a few days later with my mother and father and we were able to return to the Valentine Suite and use two different versions of the Ghost Box in an attempt to communicate. The first device we used was the Frank's Box that I had Frank Sumption custom-build for me many years ago. It's a tan-colored device about the size of a cigar box that runs on gel cell batteries. It has a small brass handle on one side and a brass latch on the other. There are two speakers on either side of the box but you can't see any of the components until you flip the lid on top open to reveal all of the dials and settings as well as an additional set of speakers. This box is by far the easiest for me to hear and relay messages. I've always felt extremely comfortable with it since the first day Frank handed it to me. While some of the other devices are clearer to the general public, this device has brought forth some of the most amazing messages. This day was no different as the girls communicated with us clearly and concisely. They stated they "loved the new owners" and even made a mention about Elaine's spiritual jewelry business. They confirmed some information that came to Joel in a dream and they also told Elaine they "loved the flowers" she brought them.

The next device we used was built by my friend Andre Wallaert and we call it the "Echo Box." This device looks like a small version of a 1930's era radio. When spirits learn to use this machine, the voices that come through sound incredibly clear. I already had some success using this device for a short time at an event held on Halloween last year. When we explained to the girls that this was a new device, they started communicating through it right away. While there was a little bit of a learning curve, we did hear the girls come through clearly several different times. Once we wrapped up our communications, I immediately started breaking down all of the EVP sessions at the office so I could share them with Joel and Elaine. I was actually able to pull more than 300 Ghost Box EVP clips out of the two recordings and shared that with them.

When I announced the Ghost Hunter University event at the Lumber Baron Inn, we sold 100 tickets in three days. We decided to add on an additional event the Friday night before, which we sold more than 70 tickets. When the Friday night came to hold our Moon Family Psychic and Paranormal Experience event, we were extremely excited to see what the spiritual response would be. My mother and I did the presentation and the attendees seemed to love it. After our gallery reading, we sent half of the group to do a ghost hunt of the property with our paranormal investigation group, the Ghost Box Paranormal

Society, while my mom assisted me with an electronic séance for the remainder of the group. The energy was great and we were able to connect several people with their lost loved ones on the other side using the Ghost Box during both electronic séance sessions.

After the event, we stayed several hours into the early morning conducting private psychic counseling/Ghost Box readings. I know the entire Ghost Box Paranormal Society team was completely drained of energy the next day from lack of sleep, but we knew we had another huge event that night. The presentation that evening couldn't have gone any better. The crowd was excited to be there and hung on every word we said. Joel and Elaine spoke a bit about who they were and how excited they were to be there. We were nervous about how to maneuver more than 100 people through all of the ghost hunting equipment stations we had set up, but once again, it seemed good energy was on our side and things went incredibly smoothly.

I was stationed with the Ghost Box in the Valentine Suite. I sat on the corner of the Jacuzzi tub with the window at my back. I gave quick instructions to each group before we went lights out in the room. From the time the lights went off, I could tell the girls were extremely eager to speak. In the first session I contacted my Technician, who identified himself by an earthly name and I heard the safe sound. I first communicated with Cara Lee and her voice came through the speakers loud and clear. I was also surprised to hear the voice of Marianne come through in a much calmer tone. It seemed her energy had settled, and she was fairly aware of where she was and who she was talking to. I was flattered when the two spirit girls "flirted" with me several times, putting me at ease.

As positive as our conversations started out, things took a very odd, dark turn. (As a result of what took place that night and in the following weeks, I have added a new element to my events and investigations—in certain circumstances, depending on the negative energy that may arise, we conduct a mandatory sage cleansing and clearing.)

As attendees respectfully asked the girls about what happened the night of the murder, strange things began to happen inside the room. From time to time a dark, negative energy pushed through and said vile things. At one point, in one of the more animated conversations, it blurted something through the speakers and then a man who stood near a piece of furniture jumped and yelled, "It just hit me on the leg!" I didn't know what he meant right away, but he explained the door on the piece of furniture next to him forcefully flew open and hit him in the leg. He closed the door and it didn't bother him again.

Once the session was over, I ran over to the piece of furniture and attempted to open the door myself, but no matter what I did, it stayed closed. Finally, I shoved my fingers over the top of the door and had to force it open. I couldn't see how the door would open on its own, let alone fly open. The night was getting interesting in a hurry.

The next group of participants came in and the messages that came through the Ghost Box become darker and darker. Finally, someone in the room blurted out, "Are you the one that killed them?"

Audibly through the speakers of the machine, we clearly heard a man's voice say, "Yesss…" Someone shrieked, as the sinister voice sounded almost like a snake.

I asked, "Are you the one who came to my event here years ago?"

There was a moment of static and fragmented noise before I heard the man's reply through the speakers, "Yeah, f**k you!" A chill shot down my spine.

The attendees, aware of the story from my presentation, began to ask the man question after question. One of the more chilling moments happened when someone asked the alleged killer, "How did you die?"

With almost no hesitation, the male entity replied, "AIDS!"

I didn't have a chance to relay what I heard because nearly everyone in the room repeated his answer. Over the course of the night, Cara Lee and Marianne verbally battled their purported killer and didn't seem intimidated by him whatsoever. It made me feel good to know the girls were strong enough to face this individual and not back down. As more groups of attendees visited the room, they informed us that the dark messages, similar to the ones we received through the Ghost Box, were being relayed through other pieces of equipment throughout the house.

We had several confirmations that night. The door on the piece of furniture flew open on three additional occasions, confirming a strong spiritual presence in the room. As we started to receive darker messages about bodies burning, serial killings, a satanic cult, and additional details of the alleged killer's death, the energy in the house rapidly turned more ominous.

The killer claimed to have brought the devil himself as well as several demons to protect him. I took this with a grain of salt as I've been threatened by these types of forces before and realize that some human spirits attempt to use the demonic to scare us away. It wasn't until one of the last groups came in that I became concerned. As a woman and her husband, both seasoned paranormal investigators, entered the Valentine Suite, the woman suddenly looked confused and it seemed as though all of the energy was ripped from her body. She turned to her husband and said, "I'm going down!" She stumbled once and then fell back into the glass shower just beyond the door. She laid there, equipment strewn around her, her husband the only one attempting to aid her.

Both Dina and I made our way across the room to help her. But being a true investigator, she insisted we continue the session with her lying there, as she knew the group had a limited amount of time to ask their questions and attempt to help the spirit girls.

After the last sessions were complete, we closed the stations and met back in the ballroom for an evidence review with the attendees. It seemed that almost everyone had some sort of deep, personal paranormal experience that night and the room was abuzz with excitement. Attendees shared their experiences and evidence with one another while we presented some of the better pictures we captured.

I was combing through evidence when one of the female attendees came up to me and asked if I would look at a picture she had taken with her camera phone. At first it didn't look like much—just three green lights far off in the background and

I didn't see much validity to it. She told me to zoom in. As I zoom in on the center green light, it became very clear to me that there was some sort of green demonic entity right in front of me. I held the phone away from me, looking closely before realizing exactly what it was. I was shocked at the clarity of this image once I zoomed in. I tried to keep my composure so as not to alarm anyone and said, "Wow! That is really interesting."

As she started to walk away, I heard some commotion off to my right. There was a group of attendees surrounding a camera phone pointing and yelling. I walked over to them and said, "What did you get?" The attendee turned to me and handed me the phone. It took me a few moments to actually comprehend what I saw. She had actually captured a true demonic form, an apparition forming and dissipating all at the same time, moving down the hall on the second floor. As I studied the image more closely, I noticed the entity had horse-like legs and hooves and there were several faces emanating from the main form. I immediately thought of the messages we received that night about the alleged killer being and his assertion he had brought demonic forces with him.

I tried not to show panic and ended the night on a positive note, thanking everyone for being a part of gathering so much amazing information in an attempt to solve the murders. Everyone had a memorable time and the house was filled with loud conversation. During all of the excitement, I'd forgotten that several people were spending the night and that I had promised I would do a public Ghost Box gallery reading for their small group before bed. I quickly grabbed my Frank's Box and gathered up the overnight group. As we entered the Valentine Suite and prepared for the session, one of the women attendees who was not an overnight guest burst into the room. She started to ramble wildly and almost incoherently. It took me a few minutes, but I finally realized she was the person involved in the demonic picture I had just seen. It looked like the entity went right through her. She seemed to be completely unaware she was walking through anything negative as she moved toward the person taking the picture, but her physical image was somewhat distorted and blurred by the demonic energy. There is a possibility the attendee may have entered some sort of vortex as she shared space with the demon.

She started asking questions and answering herself in a very strange way and then before telling us a story about how her aunt had been abducted and murdered just blocks from the Lumber Baron Inn. She said something about the killer taking her aunt to a nearby elementary school and murdering her. She said her mother could no longer go back to that school due to the bloodstains that couldn't be removed from the property. The woman suddenly came out of her excited trance and then stood quietly for the Ghost Box session.

I wondered if her aunt was a victim of the same killer as the two spirit girls in the Valentine Suite. When I ended the gallery reading that night, I told everyone to be safe and I hoped they had a great time. (In retrospect, we should have done a cleansing and blessing of the participants before dispersing.) We packed up our equipment, thanked Joel and Elaine for an amazing weekend, and made our way to my home in Louisville.

I was awakened the next morning by my iPhone buzzing incessantly. As I reached over, blurry-eyed, to see who had messaged me, I was surprised at the number of attendees who'd been contacting me regarding experiences they'd had immediately following the event. Many people complained of extreme nightmares while others had even more intense experiences. I can't say I was surprised that the three women who stayed overnight in the Valentine Suite were adamant about me contacting them regarding their experiences following the event. They told me they spent the night doing their own ghost hunt of the Lumber Baron Inn, mainly focusing on the Valentine Suite. They said they had been doing crude EVP sessions throughout the night and were surprised, during one of the sessions, to hear a sound in the room they couldn't explain. As they asked questions, they heard what sounded like a pig being slaughtered somewhere just outside the room. At first they looked for natural explanations as to what it might be. You could hear on the recording them asking if the others heard it and even checked their cell phones to make sure it wasn't a false positive. They also discussed other rational explanations such as raccoons or cats fighting outside, but when they looked through their window, they didn't see anything. Obviously, a bit shaken, they decided to go next door to another guest's room to see if anyone else had heard the sounds they had. They hadn't.

The people in the room next door said that at one point, a woman sleeping in the room sat up out of a dead sleep screaming at the top of her lungs, "Let me go!" It rattled everyone in the room—but the sound on the recorder was definitely not the sound that she made. After leaving the room next door, the women decided to attempt an EVP session in the front parlor of the house. They said that during the session, they didn't hear anything out of the ordinary, but upon review were shocked to hear what sounded like an ethereal goat bleating over the top of the women's voices as they asked questions. A bit later that night, the women decided to explore outside the mansion and were stunned to find a large cast-iron pig sculpture just outside the window of the Valentine Suite. They definitely had an interesting night.

They sent the files of the recordings to me for review and I have to admit that I'd never heard anything quite like what they recorded. As I listened to both recordings, first of the pig slaughter squeal as well as the goat bleating, my psychic senses kicked in. I was definitely sensing a truly evil presence in and around the Lumber Baron Inn.

For several days I received messages from other attendees of the event, all relaying nightmares or other strange occurrences taking place. I was deeply troubled by the power of this dark energy. One of the last messages I received was from the woman who awoke screaming that night at the Lumber Baron Inn. She told me the morning after the event, while she was getting up, she noticed a bruise on her arm and couldn't figure out where it had come from. Did she bump something? Had she slept on her arm? She couldn't remember anything and it didn't make sense to her. She said when she got home and was able to examine the bruise more closely, it looked as if someone with a large hand had grabbed her forcefully. She sent me a picture of it and it shocked me—you could see the outline of the hand and fingers on her arm. I asked her to make a video account of what had taken place and to also show the bruise from several different angles. She was kind enough to make the video and to this day

I still can't explain what happened. I've been burned, scratched, and even choked by negative spirits in the past, but this bruise was very deep and more intense than anything I'd ever seen.

I hoped to take a few days off after this event to clear my head before going back through the video, photographic, EVP, and Ghost Box EVP evidence in an attempt to pull out any information I wasn't able to decipher that night. I was also adamant about following up on the claims of the spirit through the Ghost Box of the alleged killer being dead. It was obvious to me the universe had no intention of letting me rest with matters so pressing.

I began work with one of the attendees of the Ghost Hunter University event in an attempt to track down any information on the alleged killer having died. It came back very quickly that our person of interest had, in fact, died in March of this past year, just one month prior to the event—just as the spirit had claimed.

I knew the accuracy of the Ghost Box and the amazing messages and revelations that it provides, but once again, I was completely taken aback with this validation. I thought back to when the man attended my event and it made my skin crawl. I knew how important it was for us to immediately go back to the Lumber Baron to attempt communication with the two murdered girls in hopes they could tell us if it truly was their killer—as well as demonic forces, including Satan himself—that were holding their spirits at the Inn. I contacted my team who worked the event with us. This included my mom, my wife Dina, my daughter Sarah, and Kristin, Jerrica, and Stevie from the Ghost Box Paranormal Society, as well as our tech guy. I explained to them the importance of us returning for an investigation. Stevie was unable to attend and Sarah was frightened by the intense evidence we collected that night. Surprisingly, my mother was extremely hesitant about attending the investigation and I couldn't figure out why. I called Joel and Elaine and, as always, they were very welcoming and told us we could come in and do the investigation the following night. I passed on the details of the investigation to my team that morning and that's when the strange things began to happen.

Jerrica came over to our house that morning complaining of traumatic nightmares. She said they were some of the darkest she'd ever had and I could tell she was truly frightened. After we discussed this, I rushed to squeeze in some much-needed exercise by walking my 100-pound chocolate lab Buddha. While Buddha is huge and tends to pull, I've rarely had any trouble controlling him on our walks in the past. We had walked about two miles when we turned the corner to start up the street toward my house. Buddha suddenly startled and, with all of his weight and power, lurched forward. I was caught completely off-guard and I stumbled, landing face first and palms out onto the sidewalk. Buddha stopped immediately and regained his gentle disposition, looking back at me to make sure I was all right. As I lay there, I felt blood begin to pour from my palms and knees. I didn't want to look at how bad the damage was. Eventually, I pulled myself off the ground to find skin hanging from one of my palms. I limped and had a severe pain on the right side of my ribs. I knew I had broken a rib, pulled a muscle in my ribs, or torn a muscle.

Once I got home and cleaned up, we received a call from Kristin informing us that her car refused to start. She never had a problem with the car before and couldn't figure out what was going on. She towed the car to her mechanic to see if they could figure out what the problem was. I was focused on other things and didn't realize how many things were going wrong prior to our investigation that evening. We eventually got everyone to the Lumber Baron Inn one way or another, but things definitely didn't seem right.

While standing on the porch of the Lumber Baron Inn, our skeptical tech guy said he too had experienced some very strange things. He said the night after the event he awoke in his room. He said it was so dark he couldn't see his hand in front of his face, but he also felt some sort of powerful presence staring at him. He said something along the lines of, "You're not welcome here. You need to go away." At that point, he felt a little better, but when he got up in the morning his family complained of terrible nightmares as well. I believe the threat to his family is really what bothered him and I could understand why.

My daughter Sarah drove my mother to the investigation and just before they arrived, the skies opened up and a heavy rain began to pour. I ran down to assist my mother out of the car as my daughter drove away, wanting no part of the energy at the house. When we finally reached the porch, I could tell my mom's energy wasn't what it normally was. It seemed she was susceptible to the potential darkness that waited for us inside the Valentine Suite. We had a short discussion, but decided to go ahead with the plan as we felt it was important to try to help the two spirit girls. After going over some ground rules with the team and Joel and Elaine, we decided to make our way up to the room and set up all of our equipment.

From the moment I stepped inside the door, I knew the evil energy that had harassed us was waiting and watching. It felt like all of the ions in the room were fully charged, as if something had turned on a huge battery. The air was dense and suffocating. We made our way up the staircase and into the Valentine Suite. I made a conscious effort to center and ground myself so I wasn't influenced by anything in the room. We set up our surveillance system as well as GoPro cameras and a handheld night vision video camera. While the set up was taking place, I snapped several pictures with my digital camera and saw there was already activity in the room through the spirit orbs and mists.

Once we had everything in place, I pulled out my Frank's Box as well as my digital recorder and found a seat on the edge of the Jacuzzi tub. We lowered the blinds to block the last of the daylight peeking through, in hopes we might be able to capture visual confirmation as well as Ghost Box EVP. Our team, along with Joel and Elaine, found places to either sit or stand throughout the room before starting our Ghost Box session. I rubbed my fingers together to ground myself and then flipped the silver switch of the machine. I asked for a Spirit Technician to come through and was surprised when *two* Technicians made their presence known. This told me we needed extra protection and the universe knew it.

I made the announcement to Cara Lee and Marianne that we were there to help them and were hoping to get all the information we could to finally solve this crime and bring peace and justice to them and to their families, whether it was on this side or the next. As we went around the room asking questions, the girls came through effortlessly, but were constantly interrupted by a male entity and by many bizarre growling and screeching sounds that came through the speakers of Frank's Box. While everyone asked questions, I snapped picture after picture and was amazed and disturbed at the amount of energy in the room.

I feel I've seen some incredible visual evidence in the past, but this night was different. Most of the visual activity focused around my mother and through progressively snapping pictures, I watched my mom's face contort and change into someone I didn't know. When it was her turn to ask a question, she brought up something she had mentioned to me quite a while ago that I had all but forgotten. When we first started working on the Lumber Baron Inn case, my mother told me about the murder of a good friend of hers back in 1968. The girl's name was Allison Parkins and they were in high school together. I don't remember all the details, but apparently Allison was found in her home dead, nude, and sexually assaulted with a telephone cord wrapped around her neck. I believe strangulation was the cause of death. My mom saw many similarities in what happened to her friend and Cara Lee and wondered if the same killer might be responsible for both crimes. I saw the determination in her eyes when she decided to ask Cara Lee and

Marianne's killer directly through the Ghost Box. She called out the man's name and asked, "Did you kill Allison Parkins?"

Less than five seconds went by when the reply came through the speakers of the machine clear as day. Proudly, the spirit said, "Yes, I did!"

I saw the anger and disgust on my mother's face and I'm sure everyone in the room felt the same way. He seemed pleased with his crimes. I got the impression he felt nothing could touch him in death.

I believe it was Joel who asked, "What kind of car did you drive?"

Without hesitation the spirit stated, "Blue Honda. Black leather seats." The alleged killer's spirit was brazen and he seemed egged on by the demonic forces surrounding him. Everyone in the room heard the strange growling and screeching sounds coming through throughout the session. Joel had several dreams while staying at the Lumber Baron Inn. One of these dreams may have actually shown him the face of the alleged killer. Joel asked the Ghost Box if this was the face of the killer and was given verbal confirmation through the speakers.

We wrapped up the Ghost Box session and made our way down to the porch to regroup. My mom was in some sort of daze or trance for the first few minutes we were outside, but eventually seemed to snap out of it. We decided to go back into the room with just the team and ask more direct questions of the alleged killer's spirit. We had to be quick as there was a magic show event taking place that night and people were already starting to arrive.

We raced back up to the Valentine Suite and asked some very pointed questions directly to the alleged killer and his demonic posse. The answers came through the Ghost Box quickly, almost making it hard for me to decipher what was coming through the speakers. I knew I would have to rely on my recorder to understand the sessions completely. Kristin had turned off her phone during the investigation, and when she turned it back on as we packed up, she realized she had a voicemail from her mechanic. She listened with a disbelieving look on her face. She said the mechanic could find nothing wrong with her car and that it started over and over with no issues whatsoever. It seemed something or someone was trying to stop us from returning to the Lumber Baron Inn to help these girls and solve this crime. Between Jerrica's nightmares, Kristin's car not starting, and my dog inexplicably pulling me down that day, it seemed to be more than a coincidence.

We left the Lumber Baron Inn that night a bit shaken and everyone except my mother came back to our house to have a sit-down to discuss our impressions of what took place. We all agreed it wasn't just the alleged killer's spirit that was there, but also something darker. I knew it was vital that we immediately go through the Ghost Box EVP we collected that night.

The next day Kristin and Jerrica came over to go through the recordings. I downloaded what I recorded myself and Kristin went through what was recorded on the cameras. It took us two full days to get through all of the recordings. Some of the more interesting Ghost Box EVP clips I pulled out were the voices of Cara Lee and Marianne arguing with the alleged killer. I could also clearly hear the pride he took in all of the evil he committed on earth before he died.

The demonic voices came through in many different ways. Sometimes they sounded like gibberish and I wasn't able to decipher what they were attempting to say. It wasn't until I reversed one of the clips and listened to it backwards that I started to hear clear, threatening messages. The alleged killer was happy to give details of the crime he committed at the Lumber Baron Inn and it seemed they were baiting us to come back for one last confrontation. All in all, I collected 400+ Ghost Box EVP clips from the recordings that night. In viewing the pictures we captured, I focused in on some very intriguing results. When I opened the original picture in my photo editing software, I magnified some of the spirit orbs. Inside the orbs, some of the anomalies revealed clear faces, both human and inhuman.

One of the most intense pictures I took that night was when my mother asked about the murder of her friend. Again, her face had contorted into someone else and it was obvious she had taken on another being's or entity's energy. I can't speculate whose energy it may have been; it could have been my mom's friend, Cara Lee, the killer, or something demonic. Her expression was extremely angry. Next to her face in the same picture was an extremely bright spirit orb around the size of her head. In the original picture, it appeared to be a very bright and powerful orb, but when I used a basic filter and lightened and darkened the image, it was what was inside the orb that shocked me. It appeared to be some sort of serpent coiling around what looked like a young girl's face and head. I don't know if it was a psychic impression or the clarity of the image itself, but I immediately thought of the phone cord wrapped around my mom's friend's neck and the imagery of the serpent doing the same. I was frightened.

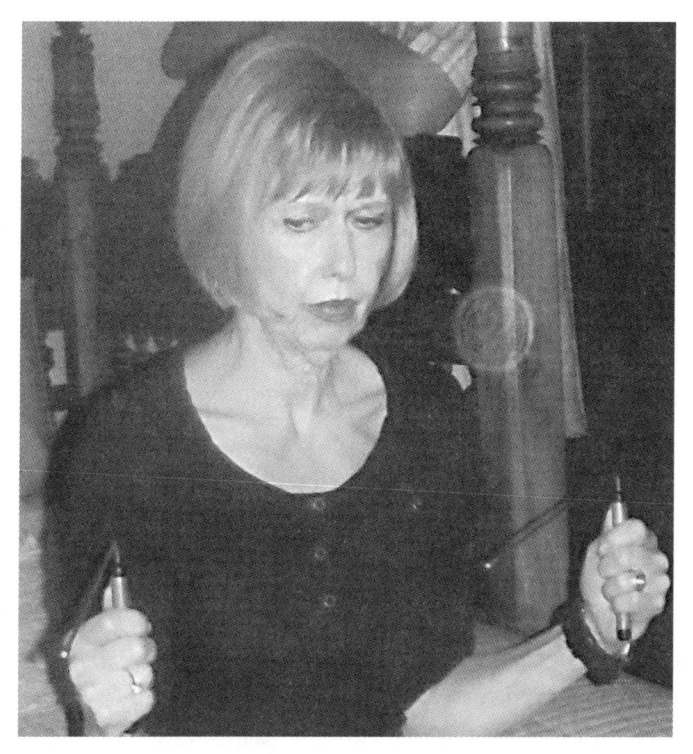

An entity appears as an orb while Paulette is communicating with spirits at the Lumber Baron Inn.

I contacted Joel and Elaine and informed them of some of the results. I told them I felt it was important we come in for one final investigation using the Ghost Box to get the last bits of information to finally solve this case. I also told Elaine I thought it was very important that, once we completed the investigation, we do a full clearing of the property. She agreed wholeheartedly.

The morning of the investigation, I went with Stevie, Jerrica, and Kristin to a metaphysical shop in Boulder to stock up on white sage for the clearing. While there, I walked the aisles of the store and came across a beautiful Christian cross that had all of the Saints metals within it. It was more of a sculpture. Most people who know me know I am not Christian. But this cross spoke to me. I realized we were battling true demonic entities inside the Lumber Baron Inn and what better way to purify the room than a cross? We went back to the Lumber Baron Inn the next afternoon. My mom decided with what happened during the last visit, she would leave the final investigation and clearing to me, Dina, Kristin, and Jerrica.

Elaine met us when we arrived at the house. We explained to her that we wanted to do the investigation portion alone as we didn't want to subject her energy to what we felt might be in the room. Elaine was gracious as always and told us she understood. The house was busy with workers remodeling and we knew we would have to work around it. Fortunately, there was no work being done in the Valentine Suite. I hadn't told the team about the crazy plan I came up with the night before for fear they might try to talk me out of it.

As they set up the GoPro cameras and night vision video camera, I announced I was going to do something a little different. I had brought four different versions of the Ghost Box and my plan was to turn them all on at the same time. I pulled out each unique device and set them in different locations in the Valentine Suite, along with a digital voice recorder over each. I planned to use my Frank's Box as the main unit while sitting on the Jacuzzi. I set the Andre's Echo Box on the piece of furniture where the door had flown open several times before. I set a newer Andre's Box, which was much smaller, black, and handheld, on the bed near the spot where the girls' bodies were found. I then set what Frank called "Sarah's Box" (he built it for my daughter Sarah, complete with a pink carrying case) on the other side of the Jacuzzi. I could sense the unease and tension in everyone in the room and I have to admit I wasn't sure what was going to happen either. I was uncertain how I would provide energy to all the devices in the room and be able to interpret messages coming through. I hoped the Spirit Technicians understood what I was attempting to do and offer the most assistance they had ever provided—but I couldn't be sure.

Once we agreed to start, Jerrica and Kristin turned on all the digital voice recorders on the Ghost Boxes as well as the machines themselves. As always, I rubbed my fingers together to ground myself and I said to myself, "I hope you know what you're doing!" I finally flipped the silver power switch on Frank's Box and slowly turned up the volume. As always, I asked for Technicians to assist and tried to quickly explain to them what my plan was. It was interesting to hear that some Technicians seemed genuinely surprised by what I was attempting to pull off. Once contact with the Spirit Technicians was established, I spoke directly to the spirit girls and told them that we wanted to solve this case once and for all and to give as much specific information as they possibly could. I then told them should the alleged killer's spirit or any demonic forces attempt to block them on one device, to jump to another Ghost Box in the room and answer there. I started the questioning and once again the alleged killer's spirit and demonic entities attempted to hijack the session. It was extremely chaotic with all of the voices coming through the different Ghost Boxes, as each one of us asked for specific information about the crime. I heard the majority of answers come through Frank's Box as it sat on my lap, but was also hearing varying replies throughout the room. At one point, Kristin felt like she was being attacked by something and she experienced extreme pain. She asked if it was the demonic entities that were causing it and was given the clear answer "yes."

I don't know if the negative energies in the room were mocking me or if they believed what they were saying, but several times they commented that "Chris is a priest."

In hindsight, I believe the negative entities knew we planned on doing a full clearing and saging immediately following this unique Ghost Box session. There were so many voices coming through the four different devices that I knew I would only be able to get distinct answers from the recordings after we finished. At the end of the session, I told Cara Lee and Marianne I loved them, to which they clearly responded, "Yay!"

I also told the alleged killer's spirit and demonic entities we were going to remove them from the property and they would never be allowed back. I ended the session and Jerrica and Kristin raced around the room to shut off each device as well as the recorders. We didn't spend time tearing down the equipment as we knew time was of the essence.

We raced downstairs to meet Elaine and told her it was time to do the clearing. Things quickly came together even though we hadn't discussed beforehand how we would perform this cleansing. I've always found it best to let the words come to me instead of reciting a rehearsed speech. I set the cross I purchased that day on the piece of furniture where the door flung itself open several times. I called out to all the entities inside the house to hear me and I dedicated the cross to Marianne and Cara Lee. I announced to all of the dark entities that had gathered in the location that they were to leave immediately and that they weren't welcome anymore.

Our team lit the white sage and Elaine lit the sweet grass before we purified every square inch of the Lumber Baron Inn. As we walked through a location, I said whatever came to me such as, "With this sage we purify this location. All negative entities must leave and never return. You are not welcome here. We forgive your trespasses and send you through to the light." Once we made a full circle and ended up back in the Valentine Suite, I reiterated everything I had said throughout the house. After extinguishing the sage and sweet grass, I placed sea salt around every entrance going into or out of the house, stating as I did, "I place this salt so no negative entities may enter this location ever again. So let it be done."

When we returned to the Valentine Suite to pack up, Elaine joined us and we continued to discuss everything that had happened. As we started to discuss Cara Lee and Marianne and where their spirits might be, a powerful feeling of calm, peace, and love filled the room. Elaine began to cry, and without hesitation, Dina embraced her. Without discussion, we knew both girls were free and could come and go as they pleased. It was an amazing feeling.

Speaking to Elaine and Joel in the days and weeks following the investigation and clearing, they reported the energy in the house as absolutely amazing. They said they haven't experienced anything negative and we were proud to have a hand in that. The cross statue remains in the Valentine Suite to this very day. After celebrating for a few days, we knew we needed to go through all of the evidence we had collected, including all of the Ghost Box EVP sessions. The idea of using the four different Ghost Boxes at the same time seemed ingenious and did work, but the downside was I had to go through four separate sessions at more than thirty minutes each. Kristin was responsible for going through the camera footage and audio of the Ghost Boxes and that appeared to be a huge task in itself.

As I started going through my sessions, I was floored at how the girls followed my instructions. If a negative entity attempted to stop them from speaking through one device, they immediately jumped to another and got the message out. It was incredible to hear and feel how empowered they were! They refused to be silenced.

Unfortunately, one thing that was clear was that the alleged killer and demonic forces refused to be silenced either. All of the important details of the crime came through the Ghost Box recordings either forward or, quite often, backward. Sometimes the information came through the recording forward and when I reversed it, there would be an entirely different message backward. It was time-consuming, but I knew I had to pull out every single voice from the Ghost Box EVP. Because this was taking such a long time, I was only able to get through a few minutes of the recordings each day. Some of the darker messages were so troubling I had to completely escape my office for long periods of time after listening to them.

Everyone on our team was starting to experience some negativity. Kristin's car began to have the same issue of not starting for no apparent reason. Jerrica's bad dreams had become chronic and were causing severe issues in her life due to lack of sleep. Dina and I experienced extremely bad luck, nightmares, and other strange phenomena inside our house. It was becoming quite the chore to go through the Ghost Box EVP recordings every day with all the negativity around us.

On my third day of working on the clips, I heard a message that shook me to the core. While I was telling the demonic entities they were going to leave the Lumber Baron Inn forever, one of them replied, "We're going to fight. Satan is coming to your house, Chris!" I've been threatened by entities before, but the voice that came through my headphones that day was legitimate. I knew the dark energy had followed all of us from the Lumber Baron Inn. More strange activity began to happen at our house right after that.

A fire alarm just outside of our bedroom door went off at 3:00 am the next morning. We changed the battery and thought it solved the problem, but the alarm continued going off at random times for a week. The next day our dog Buddha became extremely ill and threw up all over our new carpet in our bedroom and on the stairs. Strange smells of sulfur appeared just before the fire alarm would chirp again. The following morning, our small dog Bon became ill and threw up in our bed and on the carpet as well.

I knew what needed to be done. I made the decision the following night to do a full-blown cleansing of our home.

After making the decision, Dina and I watched TV on our couch downstairs. Dina dozed off and I was immersed in a show when suddenly something pounded three times on the wall beside us. Dina sat straight up and I turned my head to see what it was. Once again, we heard three loud knocks but this time they came from the opposite wall. I started to put my feet on the floor when we heard the final knocks upstairs. I looked at Dina and could tell she was extremely frightened. I stood up and ran upstairs to call out whatever entity was in the house, knowing full well what it really was. There was no response and I soon returned to the couch.

That night, again right around 3:00 am, the fire alarm chirped and had to be reset again. While reviewing Ghost Box EVP the next day, I heard an interesting message come through the headphones, but didn't understand what it meant. It was a male voice saying, "I helped Buddha. You're running out of time!" I immediately thought of Buddha in the spiritual sense but wasn't putting two and two together. That night, Kristin made the connection for me.

After listening to the EVP, she said, "Don't you get it? It's talking about Buddha, your dog…when he pulled you down prior to the investigation. It's telling you he was trying to stop you from coming!" It was at that moment I realized how serious the situation was.

I was determined to review all of the Ghost Box EVP from the Lumber Baron Inn as quickly and accurately as possible. I knew every time I played the voices through the speakers on the computer or through the headphones, the dark energy around us got stronger.

When I finished going through the last clip, I threw down my headphones and said out loud, "That's it! You're out of here!" Dina and I burned our white sage and went through every square inch of our house clearing all dark negative energy. The effect was immediate and things have been much more peaceful since.

Unfortunately, speaking to my mom that same day, she said she was having terrible luck and energy inside of her house. I made it a point to go down the next day and do a full-blown clearing of her house as well. She reports that things are much better for her after the clearing as well. Our team is now in the process of organizing all the evidence collected from the Lumber Baron Inn Ghost Box murder investigation. We believe we have definitive evidence that can solve this seventy-six-year-old crime. We plan to contact someone within the cold case division of the Denver Police Department in hopes they might be open-minded enough to take this Ghost Box evidence seriously.

A psychic's testimony isn't admissible in court. I highly doubt evidence obtained through a Ghost Box would be either. But maybe, just maybe, the voices of the victims will lead investigators to the truth.

CHAPTER · TEN

Private Ghost Box Readings, Gallery Readings, and College Tour Stories

It took me quite a while to come to terms with being a psychic medium. The stigma associated with it made me want to keep my abilities to myself or at least limited to a close circle of family and friends. Being a paranormal investigator, it was an unwritten rule to never admit you had any sort of psychic ability. If you let it slip during an investigation that you were picking up strange feelings or some sort of psychic impression, you were immediately labeled "woo-woo." I was well aware I would never be taken seriously if I were to reveal my gifts. So when I started using the Ghost Box to do private readings and gallery readings, I still had a subconscious hesitation.

When I conducted the sessions, I found myself questioning some of the words and statements that came through the speaker of the device because they didn't make immediate sense to me. I found myself censoring the information coming through and attempting to relay only what I deemed to be relevant information. While the readings were still accurate, not all of the imparted information was making its way to the client. I still remember my Spirit Technicians scolding me and telling me it was extremely important I reveal the messages just as they were.

I'm an Aries and extremely hardheaded. It took me a long time to start following this advice. Once I gave in and conveyed everything I heard coming through, the communication became much smoother for me. Different phrases and words elicited responses from my clients that I never could have imagined possible. As I relayed messages from family members who had passed away, I soon realized it was important to say things just as the spirit said them. Many times clients could hear their loved one's voice, laughter, and other personality traits come directly through the speaker of the Ghost Box. Other times it would be up to me to fill in the gaps that the spirit wasn't able to convey at that time, whether due to lack of energy or other factors.

I was once invited onto a nationally syndicated FM pop radio station morning show in Phoenix, Arizona. My grandfather had just passed away a few days earlier. The two of us were never very close or saw eye to eye on anything, so while I was sad, I felt it was important I fulfill the obligation to go on the show. When they brought me on air, it was the typical scenario for any comedy morning show, bombarding me with crude jokes and making fun of me until I cracked. I'd been in this situation dozens of times before, and had yet to give in to the scenario. They were two thirty-something DJs who seemed stocked up on caffeine when I arrived. It didn't take long for the ridiculous jokes to start and I tried to play along to the best of my ability without looking like a fool. A few minutes in, they realized they were unable to break me and told me they wanted to hear the Ghost Box live on air. They had a microphone over the top of the speaker of the Ghost Box so the audience could clearly hear what was coming through.

I made contact with my Spirit Technician and told him what we were going to do. Then the DJ said, "Yeah, I want to talk to my dad."

I asked, "What is your father's name?"

He replied, clearly trying to make me look like an idiot, "Why do you need to know that? Aren't you the psychic?"

I immediately responded, "We need to identify his energy and bring him through. What is his name?" The DJ eventually asked for his father by name and several seconds passed before we heard a faint voice come through the machine. He got a strange look on his face—I think he heard his father's voice reply, "I'm here."

The DJ jumped on this, trying to set up the punch line and make me look like a fool. With a smirk on his face he said, "My father used to have a nickname that everybody called him. If this is really you, what was that nickname?" He turned to the other DJ and said, "There is no way he'll ever get this."

I listened intently through white noise and static as well as several bits and fragments of radio that were pushing through the speakers of the box. As I was listening, I heard the DJ say, "Oh come on, I just heard our broadcast come through there!" He began to laugh with his partner. It was obvious he had no idea how this machine worked and was ready to poke holes in anything just to make a joke. I attempted to focus and continued to listen for his father to reveal the nickname. I kept hearing a specific voice coming through the speakers over and over again with one word, but I didn't want to say it.

I reluctantly admitted, "Okay, I'm hearing something but I don't think it could be right."

The DJ replied, "Yeah? What did you hear? Just say it!"

Finally, after prodding me several times, I snapped. I turned to him and said, "Pickles. He keeps saying the word pickles!"

The DJ froze. The sarcastic smile disappeared. His whole demeanor and body language changed within a matter of seconds. Realizing this meant something to him, I asked, "Does that mean anything to you?"

After stumbling on his words for a few seconds, he finally said, "Peckles. His nickname was Peckles." Tears began to well up in his eyes. After collecting himself, he said, "I need a minute" and left the booth. I realized if I hadn't relayed the word I heard, even though it was just a little bit off, he never would have had the confirmation he needed. That was a huge lesson.

The other DJ took over the show and was still determined to make a joke out of what I did. He attempted to communicate with his grandfather and armed with my newfound lesson of relaying things just as I'd heard them, I was able to connect them as well. He got a message about a truck he'd inherited and was working on. That was enough confirmation for him to know he truly connected with his grandfather. It was extremely emotional and I soon realized that there was no one talking but me on the air. One DJ had left and the other stood near his microphone but couldn't find any words.

The Box still spit out words from spirits who wanted to get their message across and I interpreted to an audience around the nation who couldn't respond. A few minutes in I heard a familiar voice come through the machine. "Christopher?"

I immediately knew it was my grandfather. I've never used the Ghost Box to communicate with my deceased family and friends. People have asked me why and I guess the easiest answer is that I just don't have a desire. I also think it would be extremely selfish of me to use it for personal communication. There are very few occasions when one of my loved ones comes through to pass along a message to me if they feel I'm in danger, but it's extremely rare and quickly passes.

So there I was, standing in the broadcast booth of one of the largest FM stations in the country, both DJs incapacitated from emotion, and my recently deceased grandfather is attempting to talk to me on the air.

"Grandpa, is that you?" I asked.

He immediately replied, "Yes, I need to talk to you."

Sheepishly I said, "Um, this isn't the best time. Can we please do this later?"

In typical fashion he replied, "I suppose!" The producer signaled they had to go to commercial and that my segment was over. I wrapped up the session and was extremely happy to leave the station that day. Looking back, it was an opportunity for thousands of people to experience something that many wouldn't have thought possible. I'm a big believer in synchronicity, and this was a great example.

I've been extremely fortunate to connect my living clients with their deceased loved ones, spirit guides, and angels. I once had a female client tell me after a particularly animated private session with her father that, "I have literally spent hundreds of thousands of dollars in therapy over the years attempting to have closure with my dead father. After paying you $120 and twenty minutes of your time, I'm completely at peace." That was an amazing compliment.

I've also experienced quite a few things I wasn't expecting. I did a Moon Family Psychic Experience at the Inner Space in Atlanta, Georgia, several years ago when the unexpected happened. We finished our presentation and my mother had completed tarot card and psychic readings for the attendees. I turned on the Ghost Box and started taking questions from the audience as always. We had some great connections in the front row and things moved along quickly. When I pointed to the first woman in the second row, she wanted to communicate with her father, but a woman's voice came through the speaker instead, demanding to speak to her. The woman in the audience became extremely irritated and said she knew exactly who the woman was and she wanted no part in talking to her. The spirit continued to force her way through the speaker and demanded she speak to this woman. The woman in the audience became enraged and left immediately after the gallery was done. She popped her head back in as we were cleaning up and said, "That was my evil stepmother who was coming through your machine. I want no part of talking to her. Why wouldn't my father come through and talk to me?"

I didn't really know what to say, as this was the first time something like this had happened, so I replied, "She must've had a message for you."

The woman replied, "Well, this is just ridiculous!"

I was a little shaken by the exchange and wondered why the Technician would allow the spirit to come through and annoy this poor woman. I shrugged it off and moved on. The next day when we returned to the shop to do a long day of private readings. I immediately noticed the woman from the night before standing in the lobby. The owner of Inner Space pulled me quickly aside and said, "She booked a private reading with you. Are you okay with that?"

I ended up doing the private reading for the woman and, while her guard was up at the beginning of the session, she soon listened to the message her deceased stepmother was trying to relay. The stepmother apologized for acting the way she did in life and told the woman she loved her very much and that she loved her father even more. The spirit told the woman that she was with her father and that he wanted to speak to her. When her father came through, he and his daughter had an extremely emotional exchange. The woman cried what appeared to be tears of happiness. By the time I turned off the machine, she seemed to have a definite sense of peace.

Afterward, she told me she was glad she was able to resolve things with her stepmother and now had a better understanding of why she acted the way she did in life. She said if she hadn't returned for the session, she never would have had closure with her stepmother and probably wouldn't have attempted to communicate with her father again. Once again,

I was glad I stuck to my guns and relayed the messages exactly as I heard them.

I've had so many incredible and emotional experiences conducting private and gallery Ghost Box sessions that there is no way I could share them all here, but I do want to touch on some that stand out to me.

As I mentioned, I've been blessed to be able to lecture, read, and conduct ghost hunts for college students on campuses throughout the United States for the past ten years. Whether it be spring, fall, or winter events, my mother and I have a busy college touring schedule. It's interesting to me that the ghost hunts on campuses seem to follow a particular pattern. Usually students go into it with the hopes to be scared, and while that does happen, what intrigues me is when they're able to experience the Ghost Box for the first time. Sure, it's cool and spooky to communicate with the spirits that remain on the campus and the students love. But the coolest thing for me is to see the reaction when a loved one in spirit comes through the speaker of the machine. It's so amazing and emotional for them that their entire demeanor typically changes. Not only does their body language change, but in most cases the vibe of the entire group of students is transformed as well. What starts out as an amped-up audience—oohing, ahhing, and laughing, ready to be frightened and freaked out—morphs into a connected group of concerned and empathetic individuals. As each student connects with their loved one, hands are placed on one another's shoulders and many hugs are shared. By the end of the night, many students come up to me with tears in their eyes, hugging and thanking me for coming to their school and connecting them with the spirit of someone they thought they'd never communicate with again. It truly is one of the greatest gifts I've ever received.

One instance on a college campus stands out above the rest. I was invited to speak at a Christian University in Lincoln, Nebraska. I really enjoy speaking at all types of schools, but from time to time, strict religious schools can be a challenge. I did my presentation for a large group of students who were extremely receptive and intrigued by my evidence and stories. When it came time to take students on the ghost hunt, there were a large number of volunteers. I'm only allowed to take forty students due to safety reasons. I had nearly double that amount on this investigation so I made an exception. We ended up going into a building I soon realized was some sort of dorm. This is not the type of building I like to be in for fear that students may want to move out after they find out there are ghosts in their campus home, but the administration gave me permission.

I turned on the device and started asking questions about which spirits were there with us. A few spirits claiming to be associated with the school came through. They gave their names and the students asked them why they were there, when and how they died, and so on. I was relaying information as fast as I possibly could, but things became a bit jumbled. Chaos is nothing new in these situations and my mother, who was there with me, tried to calm things down.

As I continued, a voice I hadn't heard in quite some time came through the speakers. I immediately knew who it was, but was afraid to relay it to the group of students for fear they would think I was crazier than they already thought. The students asked him all of the same questions and he claimed to have been a student who died there after drinking too much beer and falling out of the window. He made some jokes and everyone laughed. Someone asked what his name was and he replied, "Gus the drunk." The students laughed in unison.

I played along with him for a few minutes and then said, "Okay, what is your real name?"

There was the customary pause before he announced in full British swagger, "It's me, John Lennon!" A nervous laughter filled the crowd and then a murmur of students questioning and talking to one another. He chuckled a bit and then his voice began to fade away.

Suddenly, a young girl's voice came through the speaker and called out a name. The crowd fell silent. A young female student slowly walked from the back of the crowd toward the front. As she walked toward us, she said in a shaky voice, "What did that say?"

My mother and I repeated the name we heard. "That's my name!" she said. "I don't even believe in this stuff. I thought this was a joke."

I motioned her toward us and said, "I think there's somebody who wants to talk to you." The student stood over the device and spoke down toward it.

She asked, "Who is this?" Two distinct female children's voices came through and identified themselves. The student broke into nearly inconsolable crying. When she pulled herself together, she had a conversation with them that was heart-wrenching. It was a personal conversation I think only she could understand.

One message that everyone heard in the room through the speaker was, "Tell Mom it wasn't her fault. We're not mad at her." Again, the young woman broke into tears.

She then asked, "Are you mad at me? Do you forgive me?"

One of the girls said, "We were never mad at you." After this extremely emotional exchange, we shut down the session, and the young woman voluntarily told us what had happened. She said that some time earlier, she had an argument with her two little sisters and essentially told them she hated both of them. Shortly after, the two little girls got into the family van with their mother. Tragically, they got into a car accident. Both of the children were killed but the mother survived. The mother was heartbroken and felt responsible since she had been driving that day and their sister, the student who stood in front of us, was left with the terrible guilt of the last words she spoke to her little sisters. She was shaken by the communication we just had, but told us her sisters had come through to let her know that the accident wasn't her mother's fault and they didn't blame her. The spirits also reassured the student they knew she loved them very much.

The entire group of students was completely stunned into silence. The emotion of that moment was overwhelming for everyone present, including my mother and me. After we ended the session, we went with the girl and one of her close friends to a private conference room. I turned on the device and she was able to converse with her sisters for more than an hour. The little girls' spirits passed on messages to several members of the family. The student told us she was going to a family wedding the next day and she was thrilled she could pass along these messages to several of her family members. My mom and I both hugged her several times and told her how grateful we were to be a part of her reconnecting with her sisters. She thanked us repeatedly even as she walked away.

Of course, the topic of our conversation later that night was about this amazing communication we've been involved with. One of us turned on the television in the background and as we were talking, our attention turned to a story that popped up. It turns out it was John Lennon's birthday that day! We both looked at each other and laughed. Once again, John was a messenger and he lightened the mood before bringing in spirits who needed to relay an important message.

A week or so later, I started to receive thank-you notes from the student's family for the messages the girls relayed. They said the experience gave them all great comfort and peace, especially their mother. My mom and I felt blessed to be a part of this amazing situation.

When people think about the Ghost Box, the first thought that comes to mind is communication with the dead—however, this isn't always the case. Probably one of my most unique cases involved a favor I did for a friend. I was shopping at the mall one day when I received a call from someone I hadn't spoken to in a while. He was panicked and begging for my help. Once I calmed him down, I asked him to tell me in detail what was happening. He told me his younger brother was missing and no one could figure out where he was. He asked me to use the Ghost Box in an attempt to find out what might have happened to him, providing any possible clues.

Dina and I hurried back to the office and turned on the device. I asked for my Spirit Technician to come through and provide any information they possibly could on where my friend's brother might be, whether it be here or in the next world. When we asked for him by name, there was some confusion—he was not easy to reach. After a few minutes of intense effort, we heard a distant and strained voice come through the speaker of the machine. My friend's brother was extremely confused and my hope quickly faded away. He sounded like a spirit trapped in the earthbound realm and my goal rapidly changed from hoping to find him to doing everything I could to get him to go to the light. We talked to him for several minutes, but it was obvious he was extremely confused, as most earthbound spirits are. We encouraged him to move through the light and told him he would find peace there. At one point it sounded like he had made the decision to cross over, but we couldn't be sure.

The minute I turned off the machine, I realized I had to make a terrible call to my friend to let him know we communicated with his brother's spirit and that he was no longer with us. The phone call was extremely emotional and I felt horrible having to deliver that type of news, but there seemed to be a sense of relief for my friend. I wasn't sure I would ever emotionally recover from having to deliver that message. Eventually life and work took over my thoughts, but there is rarely a day I don't think about my friend and his poor brother.

Several weeks later I was hard at work in the *Haunted Times Magazine* office editing stories for the next issue when I received another phone call. Once again it was my friend on the phone, but this time his mood was exuberant and it was hard to slow him down enough for him to deliver the news. It turned out his brother had been in an abusive relationship and when he was reported missing, the apartment was found empty. While the police searched for him, they didn't think to search the grounds around his apartment complex. They found him behind the apartments near a stream. He was still alive, though not conscious. It seems he had been beaten and left there for several days. By the time they got him to the hospital, he was in a deep coma and they weren't sure if he would pull out of it. He was listed as a John Doe, as he had no identification on him at the time he was found. Miraculously, he woke up and soon asked for someone to contact his family and let them know where he was.

When my friend visited him in the hospital, his brother said that while he was in a coma he heard a voice telling him he would be okay and to go through the light. He said he had a vision of a man with long blond hair speaking to him and encouraging him to "go home." He heeded the advice and moved through the light and that's when he woke up. My friend was completely stunned by this news, realizing I had reached out to his brother and that I was the person he saw and heard while in his coma.

I was completely blown away by this conversation. I knew I had the ability to speak to spirits that are deceased, but I had no idea I could communicate with a spirit still in human form. This was a gigantic revelation for me. My friend didn't tell his brother about me, or that he had asked me to reach out to him. He thought it would be best left unsaid.

A year or so later, we held one of our Ghost Hunter University events at Eastern State Penitentiary in Philadelphia, Pennsylvania. My friend called and signed up for the event. We didn't think much of it other than it would be good to see him again. When the guests began to arrive at the prison, we saw our friend walking toward us with a tall, slender young man. My friend walked up and hugged both Dina and I before introducing his brother. His brother shook my hand and it seemed like a very ordinary meeting.

We conducted the event that night and after we wrapped up, I was surprised when our friend pulled me aside and said, "He told me that you are the man that he saw during the coma, the one who helped him." It was then that my friend told his brother about his request for us to use the Ghost Box to find him.

I looked at his brother who was staring at me. A slight knowing grin came over his face as he walked toward me. He grabbed me and gave me one of the tightest hugs I've ever experienced in my life. Quietly in my ear he said a simple, "Thank you." My heart was full and my head felt very light. The gravity of the situation became all too real. He released me, turned his back, and walked away. That was the last time I ever saw him. From that moment on, I realized I would always learn from this amazing machine. To this day, I don't believe we've begun to scratch the surface of what the Ghost Box is capable of.

Epilogue

What a long strange trip it's been. I've been extremely fortunate to investigate active locations worldwide. Though I've been a believer, researcher, and experiencer of the reality of an extraordinary afterlife for many years, I was not by any means someone who (initially, at least) thought Frank Sumption's creation was anything more than a broken radio. That disbelief lasted for an entire year after being given one of Frank's original Ghost Box devices to test in the field.

It was only after I actually tested the Ghost Box, first in my office and then at the Sallie House, that I realized it truly worked—and that the possibilities for using the Ghost Box were endless: connect with loved ones in spirit, communicate with historical figures from any era, and even pick up messages from diverse astral beings, from angels to ETs. Another possibility is helping the police solve crimes with the Ghost Box. My team and I are still in the process of working on a double homicide case that happened in 1970. Rumor has it the information we've provided to local law enforcement was the reason the case was reopened several years ago as an active cold case file. (My mom and I plan to write a full account of this tragic crime and what we found out using the Ghost Box in a future book.)

Frank Sumption and I worked together for many years attempting to improve the Ghost Box technology. We didn't always get along and we butted heads on more than one occasion, but in the end we remained colleagues and friends. We experienced the sudden popularity of the Ghost Box and also dealt with those who attempted to destroy the research and messages it provided.

It is only recently the paranormal and psychic communities have recognized what a great and talented man Frank Sumption was and appreciate the work Frank and I have done using the Ghost Box.

Frank passed away in 2014. Today I carry the torch for both of us in hopes of providing ultimate proof of true two-way spirit communication.

My mother and I want to thank everyone for reading our first book. We look forward to sharing many more exciting stories with you in future books! In the meantime, please visit us online:

http://chrismoonpsychic.com

http://experiencethemoons.com

https://www.facebook.com/chrismoonpsychic

https://www.facebook.com/realmammamoon

https://www.facebook.com/Psychic-Moon-Family-424448794389691

https://twitter.com/maninthemoon, https://twitter.com/PsychicMoonFam

To Write to the Authors

If you wish to contact the authors or would like more information about this book, please write to the authors in care of Llewellyn Worldwide Ltd. and we will forward your request. Both the authors and publisher appreciate hearing from you and learning of your enjoyment of this book and how it has helped you. Llewellyn Worldwide Ltd. cannot guarantee that every letter written to the authors can be answered, but all will be forwarded. Please write to:

Chris Moon and Paulette Moon
℅ Llewellyn Worldwide
2143 Wooddale Drive
Woodbury, MN 55125-2989

Please enclose a self-addressed stamped envelope for reply,
or $1.00 to cover costs. If outside the U.S.A., enclose
an international postal reply coupon.

Many of Llewellyn's authors have websites with additional information and resources. For more information, please visit our website at http://www.llewellyn.com